CW00867518

1

DISTURBARIUM

A COLLECTION OF FOUR ONE-ACT PLAYS FOR
FESTIVALS

By Emma Dinoulis

FOREWORD

These plays were written with the specific rules of the All England Theatre Festival in mind. Each is between twenty minutes and fifty-five minutes in total running time. Each has more than one speaking role.

However, I believe that they are not constrained by these guidelines; they merely allow the plays to qualify for festival entries. I believe that each play has a life of its own and its own dramatic merit. I also know, from personal experience, that they are very enjoyable to work on for performance.

I hope that, if you are reading this book, you are considering putting on at least one of these plays. If you like a mixture of dramatic dialogue and physical action, I think you will enjoy these plays.

If you would like performing rights to put on **POSSESSION, UNPROFESSIONAL BEHAVIOUR, MEETING THEMSELVES COMING BACK** or **WITHIN DOORS**, please contact rights@disturbarium.org.uk

There is a certain amount of violence in all four plays. There is also some swearing. However, I believe these are integral to the drama. They are not put in in order to shock - I believe the subjects of the plays are largely shocking enough without any need to add unnecessary content!

If you like nice, pleasant, "More tea, vicar?"-style plays, I'm afraid this collection is not for you. If you like creating an atmosphere of fear, confusion, anticipation and tension – occasionally dispelled with humour, only to be built up again – please read on!

ACKNOWLEDGEMENTS

I would like to take this opportunity to thank the people who have helped and encouraged me in writing my plays and realising the production of them.

First, I must thank Chris, my mother. An ex-English teacher, who has taught me the importance of language, you have been my guide and the spark that lit the fire.

Marian, my Drama teacher, without your encouragement and belief in me, this would not be the life-long commitment it is.

Pam, it was in one of your classes I first adapted a chapter of a novel to script form. I discovered that day that I could dramatise and I loved it.

Ann, I believe that your introduction to the violence and tension of Classical Literature and Drama inspired a certain something which has become evident in my writing. Thank you. I hope you like it.

Trevor, Anthony, Mark and Sara, thank you for forming TEAMS 5 Productions with me and thank you and Simon, Ashley and Sue for being so brilliantly instrumental in bringing the plays to life.

Trevor, in particular, thank you for inspiring three of these plays.

My last message of thanks has to go to my wonderful husband, Mark. Thank you, Darling, for all your help, support and encouragement - and for helping me to publish this collection.

POSSESSION

POSSESSION was first performed at two One-Act Drama Festivals in 2003-

The Letchworth Little Theatre Drama Festival, and

The 55th South West Herts Drama Festival at the Pump House Theatre, Watford.

The play was well received and won an award at the South West Herts Drama Festival.

Trevor D. Oakes played the role of Alasdair.

Sara Davis played the role of Suzanne.

Emma Dinoulis played the role of Ellie.

At the end of the play, it was found to be more effective on stage to have the curtain fall on Alasdair holding Ellie with his cigarette approaching her eye rather than his just holding her throat.

Lines such as "Maybe he is Juan and he just hasn't told you", worked well to break the tension with humour just enough before building it up again.

It is an enjoyable play to perform and Alasdair is a very powerful character, and difficult to break free from once you have played him!

POSSESSION
by Emma Dinoulis

[SUZANNE enters the hallway, closing the front-door behind her. ALASDAIR is sitting in the living-room, which is adjacent to the hall (both can be seen by the audience, as can part of the stairway).]

SUZANNE: [Calls upstairs] Hello!

[SUZANNE puts her door-key in a small basket on the telephone table. She puts down her bag, takes off her shoes and stands listening for a reply. ALASDAIR takes a glass of whiskey from the table by his chair and sips, silently.]

SUZANNE: [Still, listening] Hello?

[Hearing nothing, SUZANNE instinctively looks towards the living-room. She enters the living-room and stands facing ALASDAIR, who sits, watching her and sipping his whiskey.]

SUZANNE: Oh, er... hello. I'm sorry, I don't... I didn't know... I was expecting my mother to be in here. Are you... Do you know my mother?

ALASDAIR: Who's your mother?

SUZANNE: Sam... Samantha..

ALASDAIR: Where is she?

SUZANNE: Isn't she upstairs? ...Didn't she let you in? ...How did you get in?

ALASDAIR: I have a key.

SUZANNE: Who are you?

ALASDAIR: Who are you?

9

SUZANNE: I live here. This is my house.

ALASDAIR: Your house? I find that hard to believe. You own it?

SUZANNE: My mother owns it.

ALASDAIR: Then it's not your house.

SUZANNE: I live here. Who are you?

ALASDAIR: Why do you live here?

SUZANNE: It's my home.

ALASDAIR: It's your mother's home.

SUZANNE: She lets me live here.

ALASDAIR: I won't.

SUZANNE: You won't?

ALASDAIR: Why don't you live somewhere else?

SUZANNE: I can't afford to.

ALASDAIR: What makes you think you have the right to live in a house like this when you can't even afford to live?

SUZANNE: I can't afford to get a house.

ALASDAIR: Why don't you rent?

SUZANNE: It would be stupid. I'd be throwing money down the drain. I'd never be able to save for a place of my own – I'd get deeper and deeper into debt!

ALASDAIR: Getting into debt isn't a bad thing. Getting into debt isn't against the law. Buying on credit is a privilege of living in a modern, Capitalist society. Companies exist because of debt. Businesses thrive because of debt. Getting into debt is only bad when you can't pay back.

SUZANNE: I couldn't even afford to rent in this area.

ALASDAIR: Then maybe you should get out of this area.

SUZANNE: I've lived here all my life!

ALASDAIR: Then it's time you went somewhere else.

SUZANNE: I work here.

ALASDAIR: Find another job.

SUZANNE: My friends are here.

ALASDAIR: Find some more.

SUZANNE: Who are you?

[ALASDAIR puts down his glass. He takes out a cigarette and lights it.]

SUZANNE: Where's my mother?

ALASDAIR: Want Mummy to protect you?

SUZANNE: I want to know she's alright.

ALASDAIR: Why do you think she isn't?

SUZANNE: Her car's on the drive, she can't be far.

ALASDAIR: When are you going to go?

SUZANNE: What?

ALASDAIR: Get out.

SUZANNE: [Standing her ground.] I'm going to call the police.

[Pause. ALASDAIR picks up his glass and sips, thoughtfully.]

ALASDAIR: You know, you remind me very strongly of someone I don't know.

SUZANNE: What?

ALASDAIR: You remind me very strongly of someone I don't know.

SUZANNE: Well, you don't know me.

ALASDAIR: No, but it's someone else I don't know that you remind me of... Very strongly.

SUZANNE: I want you to leave.

ALASDAIR: Good! Now we're getting somewhere. You want me to leave. What else do you want? What are your other ambitions?

SUZANNE: I want you to get out of this house.

ALASDAIR: Yes, yes, we've already covered that one. What else do you aim to achieve? Of course, not all aims are achievable, but that doesn't mean you should be without ambition. You're young. Young people are our future!

SUZANNE: Would you like an ashtray? You're dropping ash all over the carpet.

ALASDAIR: Never mind that. I'll have new carpets put in soon, these are tatty, worn-out old things. I'm surprised you and your mother could put up with it.

SUZANNE: Not everyone can afford to keep changing carpets and curtains every few years.

ALASDAIR: So neither of you can afford the upkeep of the place.

SUZANNE: What is this all about? You can't take my mother's house away. She owns it. It's fully paid for. She worked for years to pay off the mortgage.

ALASDAIR: Neither of you can afford the upkeep of the place. You're the sort of people who bring down the tone of a neighbourhood. You'd rather spend money on theatre tickets than a lick of paint for the walls!

SUZANNE: I'm at liberty to spend my money on whatever I like.

[SUZANNE reaches forward to take ALASDAIR's glass. He quickly jabs at her arm with his cigarette, burning her. SUZANNE jumps back, shaking and clutching her arm.]

ALASDAIR: Aw, have you hurt yourself? Poor baby, how did you do that? Let me look.

SUZANNE: No, I'm alright.....thank you.

ALASDAIR: We must look after our young people. We must support and encourage our young people. You're our future. You're our tomorrow.

SUZANNE: You burnt me with your cigarette.

ALASDAIR: You must have brushed against my cigarette as you snatched for my glass.

SUZANNE: You burnt me deliberately.

ALASDAIR: We must look after our young people. We must support and encourage, ..and discipline our young people. You're our future. You're our tomorrow, we must make sure you're up to the job. We must make sure you can fend for yourselves before we send you out into the big, bad world! Where's your father?

13

SUZANNE: He's out.

ALASDAIR: Our where?

SUZANNE: At work.

ALASDAIR: You're lying.

SUZANNE: I'm not, he's at work. ...He'll be back soon, I
should think.

ALASDAIR: You're lying. You'd better tell me the truth.

[SUZANNE eyes ALASDAIR's cigarette, instinctively stroking
                    her arm.]

SUZANNE: I wasn't lying about him being at work, I should
think he is.

ALASDAIR: But he won't be coming back here.

SUZANNE: He doesn't live here. My parents are divorced.

ALASDAIR: I know.

SUZANNE: How do you know?

ALASDAIR: You shouldn't lie to me. ...You need a father.

SUZANNE: Do I? To protect me?

ALASDAIR: To kick you out and make you stand on your own
two feet.

SUZANNE: [Insolently.] You're doing that, maybe you
should be my father.

ALASDAIR: Call me 'Daddy'.

SUZANNE: No.

ALASDAIR: Yes.

SUZANNE: I wouldn't even call my own father 'daddy' if he was around.

ALASDAIR: Why not?

SUZANNE: Because I'm not a child.

ALASDAIR: Call me 'Daddy'.

SUZANNE: No.

ALASDAIR: You're very disobedient.

SUZANNE: Who are you?

ALASDAIR: I've half a mind to teach you a lesson.

SUZANNE: I think that's all you have got.

ALASDAIR: What?

SUZANNE: Half a mind – half a brain. You're not normal.

ALASDAIR: [Putting down his glass and starting to get up.] And you're not safe.

[SUZANNE's eyes turn to a heavy ashtray on the mantelpiece. ALASDAIR follows her gaze.]

ALASDAIR: I'd advise against that.

SUZANNE: What?

ALASDAIR: You're looking around for something to hit me with and then you intend to run. Where do you plan to go? To the hall, to ring the police? Upstairs, to find your mother? Out of the house, to take refuge with neighbours?

SUZANNE: I don't know.

ALASDAIR: No. ...I can see the thoughts rushing around your head. A light that flickers in your eyes. The adrenaline's pumping; your shallow, fast breaths make your chest rise and sink. You're shaking all over.

SUZANNE: I don't think I want to get away from you. You fascinate me.

ALASDAIR: No-one's ever talked to you like this before, have they?

SUZANNE: They haven't.

ALASDAIR: Does it turn you on?

SUZANNE: It interests me.

ALASDAIR: You know, it's half true. You're only saying it to humour me, to buy a little time to think how to get out of this situation, but it is true.

SUZANNE: That it interests me; that you interest me?

ALASDAIR: Yes.

SUZANNE: Yes.

[A pause. ALASDAIR is sitting forward in his chair, nearly touching SUZANNE, who is standing in front of him.]

ALASDAIR: You interest me.

SUZANNE: Do I?

[ALASDAIR sits back in his chair, takes a draw from his cigarette and picks up his glass.]

ALASDAIR: [Bored.] Mildly.

SUZANNE: Do you mind if I sit down?

ALASDAIR: Get me another whiskey first.

SUZANNE: It isn't finished.

[ALASDAIR drains the glass. SUZANNE lifts her arm to take the glass. ALASDAIR puts the glass on the table by his side, further away from SUZANNE, who has to reach across him to get it. She takes the glass and turns to go.]

ALASDAIR: [Grabs SUZANNE's left arm as she moves away. He draws her to him, turning her so that she is almost kneeling and they are face to face. Pause.] ...Do you have ice?

SUZANNE: I think so. I'll have to go to the kitchen for it, though.

ALASDAIR: I wouldn't try to leave the house if I were you.

SUZANNE: I don't have to leave the house to get to the kitchen.

[ALASDAIR gazes steadily into SUZANNE's eyes, not letting go of her arm. He takes a draw of his cigarette.]

SUZANNE: I thought you said you wanted me to get out?

ALASDAIR: Ultimately, yes, but not just yet. What about that whiskey?

SUZANNE: Would you like Bells or Teachers?

ALASDAIR: [Letting go of SUZANNE's arm] God, is that all you've got? ...Surprise me.

[SUZANNE leaves the room and turns towards the kitchen – away from the hall. She stops and looks back down the hall at the door, the telephone and her bag. ALASDAIR sits, smoking his cigarette and listening.]

17

SUZANNE: [Calls.] We've a little ice, only a few cubes, will that do?

ALASDAIR: [Calls back.] Whatever you have.

[SUZANNE creeps down the hall to her bag. She puts down the glass and fumbles in the bag. She pulls out a mobile phone and puts it in her pocket. She dashes to the kitchen - off stage. There are noises of a freezer door opening and shutting, ice being knocked out into a glass. SUZANNE returns to the living room with a glass full of ice and a bottle of Bells whiskey. ALASDAIR looks at her steadily and stubs out his cigarette on the chair arm.]

SUZANNE: Let me get you that ashtray.

ALASDAIR: I don't want it. Bring me my drink.

[SUZANNE approaches ALASDAIR. Pause. He takes the glass and bottle from her.]

ALASDAIR: [Undoing the whiskey-bottle cap.] Was this your mother's chair?

SUZANNE: She sits on the sofa.

ALASDAIR: [Pouring the whiskey.] Whose chair was this?

SUZANNE: I sit in it sometimes.

ALASDAIR: [Replacing the cap and setting the bottle on the table beside him.] So it was no-one's chair.

SUZANNE: I sit in it sometimes.

ALASDAIR: It's a very nice chair. I mean, it's in a nice position. It looks into the room, with the window behind you, letting in what's left of the day's sun. I can feel it warm on my shoulders and on the back of my head, like a supporting arm; a caressing hand. Look how that shaft of light plays on the surface of the whiskey – how it picks out the facets of the glass. There should

18

be a reflection or two about from the face of my watch… [Turning his wrist so that he catches the sun on his watch face.] Yes! There, look, on that wall, in the corner: in that alcove. It's darting about - a light, darting into dark recesses, exposing them.

[ALASDAIR alters the direction of the reflection so that the sun glints off his watch into SUZANNE's face. SUZANNE walks over to a chair across the room, opposite the chair ALASDAIR occupies, and sits down.]

ALASDAIR: Who said you could sit down?

SUZANNE: This is my chair.

ALASDAIR: You bought it?

SUZANNE: Yes. I bought it. It's mine. I own it.

ALASDAIR: But it's in my house. I own this house.

SUZANNE: You don't own this house; my mother owns this
house.

ALASDAIR: I possess this house.

SUZANNE: You 'possess' it? You're staking a claim.

ALASDAIR: Clever girl. …Stand up. I don't want you in that
chair.

SUZANNE: But it's my chair.

ALASDAIR: It's in my house.

SUZANNE: The house you 'possess'?

ALASDAIR: I'm staking a claim.

SUZANNE: So am I.

ALASDAIR: To what? The chair?

SUZANNE: Yes.

ALASDAIR: [Slamming down his glass on the table, standing and advancing to the centre of the room. Apparently in a rage.] Take it, then! I'll sling it out of the house! I'll throw that chair and anything else you lay claim to, and you into the street! I'll hurl you out! I'll spit you out! Your feet won't touch the ground! I'll throw you out like the refuse you are.

SUZANNE: I lay claim to the house.

ALASDAIR: [Calmly sitting down again.] The house? On what grounds?

SUZANNE: Possession. I've lived here twenty-three years. You only have to live in a place for a few years to lay claim to it.

ALASDAIR: 'A few years'? How many?

SUZANNE: I don't know exactly.

ALASDAIR: How many do you think? Guess.

SUZANNE: Less than twenty-three.

ALASDAIR: You think so? How many exactly?

SUZANNE: I don't know, I've already told you. I'm not in law.

ALASDAIR: What are you in?

SUZANNE: [Defiantly.] Not law.

ALASDAIR: Who are you?

SUZANNE: If I told you my name you'd have the advantage of me.

ALASDAIR: I already have the advantage.

SUZANNE: So you admit the game would be unfairly weighted in your favour? The scales would be tipped your way.

ALASDAIR: I think you're under a misapprehension. This isn't a game.

SUZANNE: Oh? I thought it was.

[ALASDAIR picks up his whiskey glass and drinks. He puts it down and takes out a second cigarette. He puts it in his mouth, unlit.]

ALASDAIR: Thanks for the whiskey. Lots of ice. Do you have a light?

SUZANNE: I'm sorry, I don't.

ALASDAIR: That is a pity. …I think you should give me the phone.

SUZANNE: There's one in the hall.

ALASDAIR: Don't play games with me. The mobile phone. The one in your pocket. You keep glancing towards it. The one you've got your hand on now.

SUZANNE: No.

ALASDAIR: [Taking the cigarette out of his mouth and holding it.] No?

SUZANNE: No.

ALASDAIR: [With absolute composure.] Why do you have to be so difficult? Don't you realise that, if I wanted to, I could take that phone from you as easily as …I can take a sip from this glass? Don't you understand how much stronger I am than you? [Intimately, leaning forward in his chair] Don't you see, Suzanne, that I could break your neck as easily as I can break this cigarette. [He breaks it, looking at **SUZANNE** with a charming smile, and discards it.]

SUZANNE: Why do you want it?

ALASDAIR: Why do you want it? Why did you crawl on the floor for it, scrabbling about in your bag for it? Pretending to be in the kitchen. [Tuts and shakes his head.] You're not being honest with me. I told you that wasn't wise.

SUZANNE: I wanted to have it to call the police if I needed to.

ALASDAIR: You can call them if you like, but it won't do any good. They won't be interested. In fact, they may charge you with wasting police time. That would be funny, wouldn't it? You'd call them, hoping for help and end up in a prison cell. They'd probably do you over. Beat the crap out of you. They don't like to be messed around. I don't like being messed around either.

SUZANNE: Who are you?

ALASDAIR: [Reaching out towards her, still sitting.] The phone.

SUZANNE: Why do you want to take it away from me? You've already told me I can't use it.

[**ALASDAIR** stands up, walks to **SUZANNE** with a 'no-nonsense' air and holds out his hand for the phone.]

ALASDAIR: You ask so many questions.

SUZANNE: May I ask one more?

ALASDAIR: Technically, you have.

SUZANNE: Who do you think *I* am?

ALASDAIR: I know exactly who you are: Suzanne Charlotte; twenty-three years and eight months old; mother's name Samantha Louise, father's name Juan…

SUZANNE: Juan? My father isn't Juan!

ALASDAIR: Maybe he is Juan and he just hasn't told you. They don't always.

SUZANNE: Are you from the police? …Or the government? Do you have the authority to be here?

ALASDAIR: You asked permission for one question. You'll have to make do with the answer to that, I'm afraid. Now,…

[ALASDAIR steps closer to SUZANNE and holds out his hand for the phone.]

SUZANNE: Do you mind if I put the news on? I'd like to find out what's happening in the world. There have been an alarming number of cases of police corruption and brutality recently, don't you think?

[ALASDAIR raises his hand as though to strike SUZANNE.]

SUZANNE: I suppose you're just going to keep going on about this phone until I give it to you. [She takes it out of her pocket and hands it to him.]

ALASDAIR: [Stands checking the phone.] Thank you.

SUZANNE: Did you know that smoking and drinking together is very bad for your health? Another whiskey?

[ALASDAIR smiles, puts the phone away in an inside jacket pocket, and then slaps SUZANNE across the face. A hiatus. ALASDAIR remains standing in front of SUZANNE, making it impossible for her to leave her chair. The mobile rings.]

23

ALASDAIR: [Takes the phone out of his pocket and looks at it.] Who's Ellie?

SUZANNE: I don't know.

|ALASDAIR slaps SUZANNE across the face again, no warning this time.|

SUZANNE: She's my friend.

ALASDAIR: A good friend?

SUZANNE: My best friend.

ALASDAIR: How touching. ...Isn't technology wonderful? The names and contact details of all your nearest and dearest stored on a thing no bigger than a man's fist. It wasn't even thought of twenty-five years ago – but then, neither were you.

|The mobile stops ringing.|

SUZANNE: [Her eyes tearing up.] Are you going to kill me?

ALASDAIR: Whatever gave you that idea? Not that little correction, surely? I thought you were made of sterner stuff.

SUZANNE: Why do you want to know the details of my family and friends?

ALASDAIR: I never said I did. I merely remarked that all the details of everyone you care about are on this phone. [He waves it in front of her.]

|The mobile starts ringing again. SUZANNE makes a wild grab for it. ALASDAIR pushes her back into the chair.|

ALASDAIR: [Answers the phone.] Hello? ...No, I'm afraid Suzanne isn't available at the moment. [Putting his hand over SUZANNE's mouth.] ...I think she's in the shower. Can I take a message? ...Yes, ...fine... At what time? About half an hour?

Well, I don't know if she'll be ready by then, but feel free to come round. You can always wait for her. I don't mind. ...What? Oh, I'm her uncle, sorry, I should have said! ...Alright; see you then. [He stops the call and switches off the phone, replacing it in his pocket.] She sounds like a nice girl. [He takes his hand off SUZANNE 's mouth.]

SUZANNE: What are you doing?

ALASDAIR: Playing.

SUZANNE: You said this wasn't a game.

ALASDAIR: It isn't – for you.

[A hiatus. ALASDAIR remains standing in front of SUZANNE.]

SUZANNE: You've won. I'll leave. Just tell me where my Mum is and let me tell Ellie not to come here.

ALASDAIR: You'd give up your home - your shelter; your sanctuary? So easily?

SUZANNE: It's not easy.

ALASDAIR: I mean you've made it easy for me. Stupidly easy. ...Yes, I've found the whole thing rather dull. It's hard to believe that I've broken you in such a very short time... [Scrutinising her face.] But then I haven't, have I, Suzanne? What are you planning now? Planning and plotting, scheming and calculating. What? To get away from here. To find outside help to get me out? Cut me out, like a cancer? You wouldn't find anyone who could do it.

SUZANNE: I won't challenge you; you can have what you want – possession of this house.

ALASDAIR: Maybe the house isn't all I want to possess.

SUZANNE: I haven't got anything else to give.

ALASDAIR: This house isn't yours to give. ...You're quite a feisty girl. Confident- **self-possessed**...

SUZANNE: ...'Self-possessed'? ...I don't understand you.

ALASDAIR: Oh, I think you do.

SUZANNE: I don't. What do you mean? How do you expect me to respond?

ALASDAIR: You're an intelligent girl; work it out.

SUZANNE: I think you're insinuating that the only thing I possess is myself. Are you saying you want me?

ALASDAIR: You're being too simplistic. I want your mind. Your self. I want control over you.

SUZANNE: How? Why? ...You're in control of the situation.

ALASDAIR: Not the same thing.

SUZANNE: Why me?

ALASDAIR: Why not?

SUZANNE: No special reason?

ALASDAIR: Special? [Walking away, back to the window. He stands, looking out.] What's 'special' about you?

SUZANNE: It could be anyone.

ALASDAIR: [Echoes.] Anyone. ...It might just as well be your friend, Ellie.

SUZANNE: [Suddenly angry.] Why did you tell her to come here?

ALASDAIR: I didn't. She invited herself. I just didn't prevent her.

SUZANNE: Why not? Why did you answer the phone at all?

ALASDAIR: Why not? …What are you afraid of?

SUZANNE: You. Your intentions.

ALASDAIR: [Laughs.] Strictly honourable, I assure you.

SUZANNE: [With sudden authority.] Tell me who you are and what you're doing here.

ALASDAIR: [Turning on her, cold and serious.] Don't you ever dare presume to use that tone with me.

[A long silence. **ALASDAIR** remains standing in front of the window, facing **SUZANNE**. She remains seated.]

ALASDAIR: [Casually glances at his watch. Calmly.] She'll be here in a little over twenty minutes.

SUZANNE: That's what you think! Ellie's never been on time in her life!

ALASDAIR: Really? …[With a smile.] The 'late' Ellie Simon. …So she could be twenty minutes or she could be, what? An hour? Come here.

[**SUZANNE** hesitates.]

ALASDAIR: [Sternly.] Come here.

[**SUZANNE** obeys. Rising from her chair, a little jittery, she moves unwillingly across the room to stand before **ALASDAIR**. **ALASDAIR** watches her progress.]

ALASDAIR: Exam time. This is where I find out what you know and what you've learnt from our chat, so far. What is the result of disobedience?

SUZANNE: I don't know.

ALASDAIR: Pain.

SUZANNE: ...May I ask?... ...Who classes the disobedience as 'disobedience'?

ALASDAIR: Those who are in power.

SUZANNE: And... May I ask? ...If we, who are not in power, need to question the actions of those who are in power, would this be classed as 'disobedience'?

ALASDAIR: My questions now. Whose house is this?

SUZANNE: My mother's.

ALASDAIR: [Low warning tone.] Remember what I said about disobedience.

SUZANNE: I do.

ALASDAIR: Whose house is this?

SUZANNE: My mother's.

ALASDAIR: The pain need not be yours. I'd hate to make Ellie suffer for you when she arrives; she sounds such a nice girl. I wish you were more like her.

SUZANNE: Why do you need to inflict pain on anyone?

ALASDAIR: It's the penalty for disobedience.

SUZANNE: You could be benevolent.

ALASDAIR: Oh, I am. Of course, I am. But it's been proved time and again that people need a firm, guiding hand.

SUZANNE: It's been proved?

ALASDAIR: Time and again.

SUZANNE: I suppose you want me to say this house is yours?

ALASDAIR: It is mine.

SUZANNE: I gave it up to you in return for the safety of those I care about.

ALASDAIR: It was never yours to give. You have nothing.

SUZANNE: Except myself.

ALASDAIR: Except your mind. Yes. You have learnt something! Congratulations! – I'm impressed!

SUZANNE: What do you want me for?

ALASDAIR: [Corrects.] What do I want 'your mind' for?

SUZANNE: I am my mind!

ALASDAIR: My questions now - I did say - Do you want to know more about me? What organisation I represent? My background? My name?

SUZANNE: Yes.

ALASDAIR: Good. Do you accept my absolute right to this house - and to control you?

SUZANNE: No!

ALASDAIR: Then you're not entitled to know any of that information.

SUZANNE: What?

ALASDAIR: No [sweeping past and sitting down in his chair];
you're not entitled to know.

SUZANNE: [Turning and placing herself in front of
ALASDAIR.] But if I knew those things, it would inform my
judgement about your right to this house.

ALASDAIR: And to your mind... If you don't acknowledge
my authority, you can't have my information. ...By the way
[Intimately, leaning forward in his chair], don't talk about 'your
judgement'. You have no judgement.

SUZANNE: You're expecting blind obedience without giving
me any justification for your position of power. Why should I do
what you say?

ALASDAIR: [Sits back and picks up his glass of whiskey.]
Let's be frank; do you have a choice? [Sips his whiskey
thoughtfully, for a while.] ...I want to show you something. [He
replaces the glass on the table and pats his jacket pocket; at last
finding what he wants.] Ah, yes, here it is! Come closer. Take a
look.

[SUZANNE closes in more. At indications from ALASDAIR, she
bends slightly to look at what ALASDAIR draws out. It is a hand-
held electric stunner. It crackles. She straightens and backs away
slightly.]

ALASDAIR: Hisses like a snake, doesn't it?! Have you heard
of the Taser M26 stun gun?

SUZANNE: I have. I've read and heard quite a bit about it.

ALASDAIR: A subject on which you're informed! What do
you know about it?

SUZANNE: The advanced Taser stun gun has just been
approved for use by the police. They say it will only be used in

30

situations where guns would have been deployed before. We do not believe this to be the case.

ALASDAIR: You suspect wider use?

SUZANNE: There are precedents.

ALASDAIR: Go on. What do you know about what it does?

SUZANNE: It has a range of thirty feet. When it is operated, it fires two metal barbs into the victim's body.

ALASDAIR: [Corrects.] Into the suspect's body.

SUZANNE: It can penetrate up to two inches of clothing to hit the body. The victim... the suspect is then disabled by a charge of fifty-thousand volts. Involuntary defecation may occur. He or she falls to the ground, paralysed, and remains incapacitated for up to fifteen minutes. He or she may lose their memory.

ALASDAIR: This isn't a Taser M26, as you probably know. This is an older model, a predecessor – you might say this is the Taser's daddy; or uncle, as it's not quite the same sort of weapon. Not as powerful, perhaps, but its use can be repeated until the desired effect is achieved. It's used at close range – not a weapon for cowards.

SUZANNE: It's cowardly to use a weapon of any sort on someone who's unarmed.

ALASDAIR: I'm sorry, did I hear you venture an opinion? Were you moralising? Sermonising? Holier-than-thou-ing?

SUZANNE: I was voicing a ...casual thought.

ALASDAIR: Who mentioned using it on anyone unarmed?

SUZANNE: Why are you showing it to me?

ALASDAIR: Because now you know that I have it. ...Back to the exam. Well done on the Taser section of the test, by the way, very informed – very well put!

SUZANNE: Thank you.

ALASDAIR: ...If you ignore the sentimentality that creeps in every now and then – here and there.

SUZANNE: Can I hold it?

ALASDAIR: What? [Making the stunner crackle.] This?

SUZANNE: Can I?

ALASDAIR: What for? [Laughs.] Thinking of using it? [He hands her the stunner.]

[SUZANNE takes it. She pulls the trigger and it crackles. ALASDAIR sits back in the chair and goes back to sipping his whiskey. SUZANNE points the stunner towards ALASDAIR and makes it crackle. ALASDAIR puts down his glass and gets out a cigarette.]

ALASDAIR: Have you got a light? [He seizes SUZANNE's hand and brings hand and stunner towards his cigarette. He lights (or pretends to light) his cigarette with it.] Thanks. [He smiles; lets go of SUZANNE's hand and sits back in his chair, observing her.]

[SUZANNE stands, holding the stunner. PAUSE.]

ALASDAIR: Have you finished with that?

[SUZANNE continues to stand, holding the stunner, looking at it, then at ALASDAIR.]

ALASDAIR: Time is ticking away, Suzanne. Ellie will be on her way. Has she got a mobile phone? ...No? You won't be able to reach her now, then. If she's left the house.

SUZANNE: She has got a mobile.

ALASDAIR: Ah. ...And her phone is always switched on? Can you always reach her if you need to? ...Or is she one of those annoying people you can never get hold of? Always on voicemail. A robot voice; a machine; no understanding; no human contact; impossible to move; deaf and dead. Why do they bother having a bloody mobile if they never intend to answer it? ...Why don't you give me that back?

SUZANNE: I... No!

ALASDAIR: You're not going to use it.

SUZANNE: I will if I have to.

ALASDAIR: Try.

[Tense pause, then **SUZANNE** turns away and makes to leave the room.]

ALASDAIR: Where do you think you're going?

SUZANNE: Upstairs. ...I need to use the toilet.

ALASDAIR: You can stay here and piss yourself.

SUZANNE: Fuck you!

[SUZANNE leaves the room and ascends the stairs. ALASDAIR stands up slowly and turns to look out of the window. He watches for a moment, then waves. He leaves the living-room and walks down the hall to the front door. He lets ELLIE in.]

ALASDAIR: [Extremely affable.] You must be Ellie! Come in. Suzanne's just upstairs. I'm sure she won't be long.

ELLIE: Thanks. Sorry, I'm a bit early. I thought I'd have to walk but Dad gave me a lift.

ALASDAIR: That's lucky, isn't it! [Walking into the living room.] Would you like a drink? I'm on the whiskey, myself. Fancy a nip?

ELLIE: [Following **ALASDAIR** in.] No, I'm fine, thanks. I don't really like whiskey.

ALASDAIR: Not surprised! Filthy stuff, really! [Sitting down in his window chair and gesturing towards the sofa.] Please make yourself comfortable.

ELLIE: [Sitting down.] Thanks. So, you're Suzanne's uncle?

ALASDAIR: That's right. Uncle Harry.

ELLIE: It's funny I've never met you before.

ALASDAIR: Well, I don't live nearby. …And I travel a lot... Abroad. You're Suzanne's best friend?

ELLIE: Yes. We've known one-another for years. We were at school together.

ALASDAIR: Did you go to the same University?

ELLIE: No, but we stayed in touch the whole time.

ALASDAIR: Really? You must know more about my niece than I do.

ELLIE: Probably.

ALASDAIR: What sort of things do you talk about?

ELLIE: Oh, life, work, stuff like that…

ALASDAIR: Boyfriends?

ELLIE: Sometimes.

ALASDAIR: Has she got a boyfriend?

ELLIE: Not at the moment, I don't think. Why do you want to know?

ALASDAIR: Just curious... Be nice to have something to tease her about!

ELLIE: [Brightening up.] Oh, well, you could pretend there's a conspiracy going on!

ALASDAIR: [Amused.] A conspiracy?

ELLIE: Yes. It started when we were on the phone one day, talking about politics, or something. There was a noise. A click,... on the line. We had a laugh about it. Said we were being bugged! Of course, if anyone did listen in to our conversations they wouldn't get any sense out of it!

ALASDAIR: [Amused.] I bet you were being bugged! Were you talking about anything controversial?

ELLIE: I don't know what we were talking about. Probably. It usually is!

ALASDAIR: Come over here. I want to show you something. It's a picture of Suzanne as a baby. Well, a toddler really. It was when I saw her last.

ELLIE: [She gets up and goes to him.] Oh, really?

ALASDAIR: [Standing with **ELLIE** he gets a photograph out of his jacket pocket.] Yes. Look, she's hardly changed! [Laughs.]

[Behind them, **SUZANNE** descends the stairs, stunner still in hand. She looks towards the living room then towards the front door. She pauses on the last step.]

SUZANNE: [Calls.] She's not upstairs. I don't think she's even been back since this morning. I'm going now. Do what you like!

ALASDAIR: [Calls back.] Come back in here for a second, Suzanne. There's someone here for you.

[SUZANNE **enters the living room to see** ALASDAIR **standing behind** ELLIE. ALASDAIR **puts his hand on her throat.**]

END

UNPROFESSIONAL BEHAVIOUR

Although the most recently written play, **UNPROFESSIONAL BEHAVIOUR** is published second in this collection as it shares a character with **POSSESSION**. Mr Church is none other than an older Alasdair.

It is likely that, if it were necessary to perform two one-act plays from this anthology back-to-back, **POSSESSION** and **UNPROFESSIONAL BEHAVIOUR** could make an ideal double-bill.

UNPROFESSIONAL BEHAVIOUR would work best for an audience familiar with **POSSESSION**, using the same actor to play Alasdair in both plays. Although this would be demanding for the actor, it could prove a true tour de force!

Unprofessional Behaviour
by Emma Dinoulis

Cast

Mr. Church - A retired man in his 70s. Grey haired and with a walking stick, Mr. Church gives the impression of vulnerability and infirmity. However, one can see that he has a large build and has been very strong.

Jenny - Jenny is a young woman in her 20s. She is attractive and can be sexy but not particularly slight in build. She looks as though she can handle herself, physically, and she is quite self-sufficient. She wears jeans and a t-shirt or similar clothes – casual but in keeping with working as a carer.

Paul - A strongly built man in his late 20s or early 30s. He is arrogant and self-satisfied, believing himself more intelligent than he is. He wears combats, a t-shirt and boots, all spattered with paint. He is little more than a thug, although he stands upright and walks with confidence.

Scene
Mr. Church's flat

Mr. Church lives in a large, simple flat. It is tidy to the point of obsession except for a number of whiskey bottles, which stand and lie about the floor in various states of emptiness. The furniture is simple and functional. There is no television, only a radio/CD player, which is on at the start of the scene. There are books on a bookcase by Mr. Church's chair. The books cannot be seen as the bookcase is back on to the audience. Mr. Church's arm-chair is side on to the audience, cheated slightly further round to face them. He is left and front of centre stage. There is a door centre back. This is Mr. Church's front door. There are exits stage left and stage right, into the kitchen and bathroom, respectively. There is a suggestion that Mr. Church's bedroom is towards the audience.

[**Mr. Church** sits in his armchair, in contemplation, sipping
whiskey from a glass. His walking stick is by his side, tucked
into the seat of the arm-chair. The radio is on.]

Sports Commentator: [*On the radio*]   They're at the
starting post, now. The jockeys are lining them up. Trouble with
Seathelight; he's turning at the tape. The official has raised his flag;
he's ready to start the race. Connell gets Seathelight under control.
They're off. It's Stargazer from Lindie's Lad; Igotwings tucked in
just behind. Seathelight's breaking forward despite a slow start.
Fiery Fred and Rampart are neck and neck, leading the next group.
That's Fine Filly, Jackthelad, Diablo and, trailing at the moment
from the front of the field, are Royal Purple, Worldbeater, Sexy
Sioux, Eatmydust, Fallen Angel and Jet Black.   Seathelight's
coming through to lead the field. Might be too early to come in
front at this stage. Time will tell. The leaders are coming up to the
first jump. Seathelight from Stargazer. Igotwings is over, then
Lindie's Lad. Fiery Fred has just got clear. Rampart's over but
he's landed in the path of Fine Filly. Fine Filly's over, might have
caught Rampart as she landed. They're running on but Filly
overtakes Rampart. Jackthelad, Diablo and Fallen Angel are next –
Fallen Angel making a sudden break from the back five. They're
all over the first fence. The leaders of the field are coming up to the
second: Seathelight, Stargazer, Igotwings still through from
Lindie's Lad. Fiery Fred's refused – Jacobson's off. He won't be
happy with that finish after last year's Grand National! Fine Filly
from Rampart.   Diablo and Jackthelad come over the second
together.   Then it's Fallen Angel, Royal Purple, Worldbeater,
Eatmydust just ahead of Sexy Sioux. Jet Black's thrown his rider
but he's running on.   At the front of the field, Stargazer and
Seathelight are together with Igotwings just a nose behind. Lindie's
Lad is being pushed by Fine Filly. Fine Filly's passing Lindie's
Lad.   Fine Filly's just a few strides behind the leaders, now.
Jackthelad, Diablo and Fallen Angel are making ground on Lindie's
Lad. Jet Black looks like he could be a problem at the next jump,
he's staying with the field…

[**The doorbell rings. Mr. Church does not show that he has
heard it. He continues to listen to the radio. There is a short
pause before the doorbell sounds a second time. Mr. Church**

looks towards the door but does not get up or put his whiskey glass down. Another pause while the radio commentary continues. Then a knock at the door.]

Jenny: [Knocking and calling through the door] Mr. Church? Can you let me in, Mr. Church? Can you hear me? Christ, that radio's on loud! Mr. Church? Can you hear me?

Mr. Church: [Turning the radio commentary down slightly using the remote control] Who is it?

Jenny: My name's Jenny. The council sent me... ...To look in on you – see if you're OK? See if you needed anything doing for you?

Mr. Church: I'm fine! Piss off! [Turning the radio commentary back up.]

Jenny: [Quietly] Stupid old bastard!

Mr. Church: [Turns the radio off and looks mildly amused. Pause.] You're still there, aren't you.

Jenny: Yes, Mr. Church. Open the door.

Mr. Church: Why?

Jenny: I have to *see* you're alright. I can't take your word for it.

Mr. Church: Why not? Because I'm old? Because I might be senile? Off my rocker? Unable to tell whether I'm perfectly fine or not? In need of some little girl to ascertain that for me?

Jenny: Yes.

Mr. Church: [Again mildly amused.] What? [He puts down his glass, takes up his walking stick and moves himself towards the front of his arm-chair seat]

Jenny: Yes. You might be senile. You might sound OK but be in a state in there. I don't know, do I? Unless I see.

Mr. Church: What are you wearing, Jenny?

Jenny: What's that got to do with anything?

Mr. Church: Deciding if *I* want to see *you.*

Jenny: What are you? An old perv? I'm naked... ...if that'll make you open this door any quicker.

Mr. Church: You're not naked...

Jenny: D'you reckon?

Mr. Church: ...And you don't work for the council.

Jenny: Let me in, Mr. Church.

[Mr. Church walks awkwardly over to the door, leaning heavily on his walking-stick.]

Mr. Church: [Looking through a spy hole in the front door] Step back from the door, Jenny.

Jenny: Why, Mr. Church?

Mr. Church: I want to see who's with you.

Jenny: There's no-one with me.

Mr. Church: [Seductively.] You'd better not be fibbing. Little girls who lie get spanked in *my* house.

Jenny: [Matching Mr. Church's tone] *I'm* not a little girl.

[Mr. Church opens the front door a crack and steps back, away from it. Jenny slides her way in. Mr. Church attempts to push the door closed but is sent backwards by the door hitting him as

Paul forces his way in. Jenny kicks out Mr. Church's stick from under him so that he falls centre stage with head towards the audience. His walking stick falls next to his armchair.|

Jenny: See, you were wrong – you're not alright. Guess you must be gaga after all.

Paul: [To Jenny] Lock the door.

|Paul leaves Jenny standing by Mr. Church, who is still sprawled on the floor. During the next exchange, Paul walks into the bathroom (exiting stage right), and the kitchen (exiting stage left). There are the sounds of an untidy search.|

Mr. Church: [To Jenny] But I was right - you were lying.

Jenny: Oh yeah. D'you want to spank me now or later?

Mr. Church: Later will do.

Jenny: [Standing over Mr. Church in a sexy but aggressive manner] Don't think you're in any position to choose, now, do you?

Mr. Church: Don't hurt me, Jenny, will you? Don't let your ...friend, hurt me?

Jenny: Are you scared, Mr. Church? Are you scared of me? Wasn't I just a little girl, when I was the other side of that door? ...And when I first came in. I saw the look on your face, you dirty old bastard! [She walks closer to Mr. Church, pushing him to move back, away from her. Smiling.] I like having men at my feet. ...Not that you could *do* anything. Could you? You're just a harmless old man. Aren't you?

Mr. Church: You're right.

Jenny: Say it, then. Say, "I'm just a harmless old man, Jenny."

44

Mr. Church: I'm just a harmless old man, Jenny. You're right. I can't do anything to you. I'm completely in your power. Please don't hurt me. Is it money you want?

Jenny: It's money *he* wants. [Indicating Paul with a toss of her head.]

Mr. Church: And what is it *you* want, Jenny?

Jenny: I think you know what I'm getting out of it.

Mr. Church: I think I do.

[Paul comes back to Jenny, interrupting what is becoming a flirty conversation with Mr. Church.]

Paul: [Again to Jenny] Lock the fucking door. [Stands over Mr. Church.]

Jenny: Alright. [Goes behind Mr. Church and Paul to the front door. She looks at it and fiddles with it for a while during the next exchange.]

Paul: [To Mr. Church] Where's your money?

Mr. Church: Do you mind if I get up?

Paul: [Kicking Mr. Church in the stomach] Where's the money, Grandad?

Jenny: I can't.

Paul: Can't what?

Jenny: Lock the door. It's weird. It's not like a normal one.

Paul: Don't be stupid. It's just a fucking door.

Jenny: Well, I can't do it. Look. You try.

Paul: Useless bitch! You watch him.

[Jenny moves forward to watch Mr. Church. He is writhing on the floor, bent double after the kick to his stomach. He coughs. She passively observes him as though fascinated by his pain. She moves round to see his face. Paul moves to the front door and looks at the locks. His initial confidence quickly leaves him. He tries the door and finds that it is already locked.]

Jenny: [Lifting Mr. Church's head by the hair] What's your first name?

Paul: [Coming back to Jenny] What are you doing, chatting him up?

Jenny: Sorted the door?

Paul: Yeah, it's locked.

Mr. Church: [Pulling himself onto his arm-chair] Clever boy! And, of course, you know how to unlock it again.

Jenny: [Getting in between Paul and Mr. Church to stop Paul attacking Mr. Church again] What is with your door, Mr. Church? I've never seen a lock like that.

Paul: Fuck the door! Where's your money you old...

Jenny: [In a whisper to Paul] Might be a good idea to know how we're getting out of here afterwards, don't you think?

Mr. Church: Clever girl, isn't she, Paul.

Paul: Don't need a door – we'll smash a window.

Jenny: Paul?

Paul: What?

Jenny: He called you Paul.   …How d'you know his name?

Mr. Church: You can try to smash the windows but they're bullet proof.

Paul: How d'you know my name?

Mr. Church: Your girlfriend whispered it in my ear while you were at the door.

Jenny: [To Mr. Church] How do we get out?

Paul: What's wrong with you? You fancy this walking corpse?

Jenny: What? I'm trying to get us a way out, you tosser!

Mr. Church: I wouldn't stand for that, Paul. Bad enough that she whispers in my ear and flirts with me but insulting you, too, making a fool of you in front of me…

Jenny: Shut up!

Mr. Church: You can't be very good in bed if your whore's hitting on a seventy year old, can you.

Paul: I'll fucking kill you if you don't shut up!

Mr. Church: Don't you want my money, Paul? Don't lose your focus or you don't know what might happen. …It's in my bedroom [gestures towards the audience, stage left]; under the mattress. Not very original, I know, but you know us old fogeys.

[Paul starts to move towards the bedroom.]

Mr. Church: Are you going to leave us here together? What do you think you'll find when you come back? Do you think she'll be fucking me? I don't think you appreciate what a sensual creature she is. It oozes out of her. I knew it as soon as I heard her through that door. Even her voice is a dead giveaway. She wants someone to take her and bang her brains out. ...Shame you're not that man!

Jenny: [To Paul who's frozen in fury] Just get the fuck on with it, Paul! Go and get the money. I'll get him to tell me the way out.

Mr. Church: Don't ride me too hard, Gorgeous! I'm not as strong as I used to be!

Jenny: Shut the fuck up! [To Paul] You're not listening to this old perv, are you? You are! You're thick as shit! How fucking jealous are you? Go and get the fucking money and let's get out of here.

Mr. Church: What makes you so insecure, Paul? Is it the size of your dick? Or is it that she's so powerful, she keeps your cock in her handbag?

Jenny: [Confronting   Paul] Yeah, that's it! He's shit scared because I'm smarter than him and he's got to show how big and fucking macho he is. Look at him, standing in that doorway, the money's right under his fucking nose and he's letting the senile drivelling of an old cock-sucker shake him. He's pathetic! He's fucking laughable!

[Mr. Church takes his walking-stick and swings it round his head, cracking it across the back of Jenny's skull, felling her to the ground. Paul has registered rage and jealousy until this point. Now he is lost for a reaction.]

Mr. Church: Don't worry, she's not dead: only unconscious. ...Or don't you care? ...Would you rather I'd left you to hit her? Sorry to take that away from you. But I don't believe you've knocked this one around, yet? I'm sure you've had no trouble slapping other girls about – but this one's different, isn't she. You need to, you know – put her in her place. If you don't teach her soon she'll have you – there [gesturing under her thumb]. ...Not much of a conversationalist, are you. Would you like some whiskey? Oh, I know you're already lagered up to do the job – bad idea, incidentally, you should always keep a clear head, during. Just use the drink to blot it out after – or to revel in it. Come on. Come back. Stop loitering in my bedroom doorway; you're making the place look untidy. Go and get the money or come here, sit down and have a whiskey with me, Paul. That's the choice. ...You're honoured, by the way, I don't usually give people a choice.

Paul: How much money have you got?

Mr. Church: [Correcting him] *Mr. Church*.

Paul: [Approaching Mr. Church swiftly and aggressively] You're playing a dangerous fucking game with me.

Mr. Church: [Holding his walking stick as thought it's a swordstick he's about to unsheathe] I wouldn't.

Paul: [Stopped in his tracks] That's only a walking stick.

Mr. Church: Can you be sure? From that distance? You were saying. "How much money have you got, *Mr. Church*?"

Paul: You're an old wanker.

Mr. Church: I'm also an old man who, not so long ago, earned his crust removing those who had become... an irritation - and you can afford to show me some respect, sit down and have a drink with me.

Paul: An assassin?

Mr. Church: If you want to call it that, yes. Well done: you and your girlfriend here [indicating Jenny, still lying on the floor, unconscious], have managed to break into the home of an assassin.

Paul: There are no assassins outside films and books. What d'you think I am, stupid?

Mr. Church: Yes, I think you're stupid. I didn't initially – I thought you were lagered up, a bit hen-pecked and jealous but sensibly quiet and focussed. Now you're starting to disappoint me. You bore me. I hate boredom!

Paul: You don't talk like an ordinary old geezer.

Mr. Church: [Sarcastically] I'm flattered.

Paul: Are you really an assassin? I mean *were* you?

Mr. Church: For fuck's sake! Yes.

Paul: [In awe] I'll have that drink with you, Mr. Church.

Mr. Church: [Surprised at Paul's sudden change] Good. There are more chairs in the kitchen. Why don't you get yourself one.

[Paul exits stage left.]

Mr. Church: [Calling to Paul] Bring yourself a glass and bring us ice from the freezer while you're there.

[While Paul is out of the room, Mr. Church moves so that he is bending over Jenny. He lifts her head by the hair, checks her breathing and then lowers her head again. Mr. Church returns to the position in his chair he was in when Paul left the room. Paul enters carrying the kitchen chair a glass and a tray of ice. He looks awkward and in danger of dropping everything.]

Mr. Church: What a shame Jenny can't join us for a drink.

Paul: [Looking down, amused and vindictively at Jenny who is lying between him and Mr. Church] Maybe we could pour some down her throat.

Mr. Church: If you want to. It might bring her round, though, and I was enjoying her having her mouth shut!

Paul: [Laughing conspiratorially] Yeah, she's always at it. Fucking jawing all the time.

Mr. Church: [Seriously. Taking a half-full bottle of whiskey and unscrewing the lid.] Glass.

[Paul gives Mr. Church his glass.]

Mr. Church: [Pouring a large measure in first his own and then Paul's glass] Why don't you teach her a lesson? Ice.

Paul: [Giving Mr. Church the tray of ice] What d'you mean?

Mr. Church: [Putting ice into the glasses and handing Paul his over the top of Jenny, but not letting go of the glass.] While she's not in control. Set everything up so that you've got the upper hand. Keep her vulnerable. Keep her submissive. [Releases the glass and lets Paul take it.]

Paul: How?

Mr. Church: Cheers! [He drinks.]

Paul: [Drinks] How?

Mr. Church: Good, smokey bite to this whiskey, don't you think? I used to smoke. I gave it up when my doctor told me it'd kill me in a very short time if I didn't. Foolish of me. If I'd thought for one moment I'd end up here I'd have done everything to keep my life short and thrilling. Danger and death – violent death – are so sweet. There's no drug like it. Torture. The beautiful vulnerability of terror in tear-filled, pleading eyes. You've tasted that – just a little. Are you hungry for more?

Paul: Tell me how, Mr. Church. You know I'll listen. You've chosen me, haven't you? To learn about stuff from you? I want to learn. I'm more than a thief. You know that. You saw that in me – you've said. What d'you want me to do?

Mr. Church: Give me your glass. [Taking it, filling Paul's glass and his own and passing Paul's glass back to him] Drink it. ...I shouldn't tell you any of this.   It would be considered "unprofessional conduct". I'll teach you. I'll take you through the skills. You're right. I've chosen you. I've no-one else to pass my knowledge on to – no son. I'll be dead soon. I'd be sorry for my art to be lost. ...Go and get another kitchen chair. There's a roll of duct tape in there, too – second drawer down in the sideboard to your right as you go in. Bring them.

[Paul obeys, exiting stage left. While Paul is out of the room, Mr. Church picks a book off the bookshelf and opens it to reveal that it's a storage box. He takes out a hand-held stun gun. He reaches down under his chair and takes out a handgun. He opens it, checks for bullets and locks it again with a click. He places both the stun gun and the revolver on top of the bookcase, by his armchair. Paul returns with the chair and duct tape.]

Paul: [Setting down the kitchen chair centre stage, behind Jenny and between Mr. Church's arm-chair and his own chair. He places the duct tape on his own chair and looks down at Jenny.] I know what I do now – I put her on the chair and tape her to it, right? I've seen this in films.

Mr. Church: Very good. Wrong. But imaginative. Take her while she's on the ground. Make your life easier. Tape her arms behind her back. Turn her onto her side and tape her ankles and knees together. You don't know how soon she'll come round. Save time. Keep the advantage. ...Well, what are you waiting for? Do you want me to do it?

Paul: [Slightly embarrassed.] No, no. [He takes the duct tape and kneels by Jenny. He takes her wrists in his left hand. He pauses. He grins up at Mr. Church.] This'll really hurt when she takes it off.

Mr. Church: [Suddenly harsh, hard and commanding] Forget it, then. If you're too soft to tape her wrists you're too soft for any of this. I wash my hands of you. You common, petty burglar. You

52

ignorant, cowardly turd. Fuck off back to your mummy. Take the money and run away, little boy.

Paul: [Mortified] No, no, I didn't mean... I'm sorry. I can do it. I'll enjoy it. [He holds Jenny's wrists in his left hand but can't start the duct tape off using only his right.]

Mr. Church: Stop. Do everything as I tell you.

[Paul does everything as Mr. Church commands.]

Mr. Church: Let go of her wrists. Put the duct tape down. Kneel on your left knee and put the right across the small of her back. Pick up the duct tape in your left hand and start it off with your right – about three inches. Keep hold of the loose tape in the fingers of your left hand while you grab her right hand and pin it with your right knee. Grab her left hand and put it over her right. Hold her hands with your right hand and tape her wrists together now. Good. Rip it. Now, take her right arm with your left hand and her right thigh with your right hand and pull her towards you until she's on her side, leaning against your knee. Change to kneeling on your right knee and support her with your left knee. Pass the tape under her thighs, just above the knee. Tape it good and tight, Paul. Now her ankles. Good. Now put her on the chair. Put her on her stomach. Put your arms through hers and lift her. ...Come round to the front and lift her so that her arms are behind the back of the chair. Now. Want to wake her? Reveal to her that she's at your mercy? [Looking hungrily at Jenny] Absolutely defenceless. Utterly vulnerable. Very much ...in trouble.

Paul: Yeah I'll slap her.

Mr. Church: [Secretively] You *can*, of course...

Paul: What else?

Mr. Church: Sit down, Paul. Your lessons have only just started. Don't you want to know absolute control? Do you really want to wake Jenny only for her to see you taking orders from a "walking corpse"?

[Paul sits, obediently. Mr. Church picks up the stun gun. He stands without his walking stick. He walks, shakily but steadily to Jenny. He stands behind her.]

Mr. Church: This is a subtly adapted Streetwise 600,000 volt stun gun. I've disabled the alarm and tweaked up the effectiveness. The voltage is a little over average for this kind of weapon. You *can* kill with it. I prefer to use it only for pain. It has most effect, I have found, when applied directly onto the skin and in the soft, fleshy areas of the body. [Demonstrating the areas as he mentions them, putting the stun-gun to the part but not pushing the button.] Here, at the side, under the rib cage. Here, the stomach, around the diaphragm. The obvious places, as well, of course. ...And, if you're near the end of the conversation and don't much care if she lives or not, there's always the throat. Use it at arm's length. Watch the head – they can thrash about when the current's surging through them.

[Mr. Church returns to the bookcase and replaces the stun-gun on the top. He takes the revolver and stands, holding it and looking at Paul.]

Paul: We're not going to kill her, are we?

Mr. Church: *We're* not going to do anything. The choice is yours. Could you kill her if you had to? She's not important to you – is she? You can't have ties if you're an assassin, Paul. ...Could you kill me? You could have done when you first came in. You hit me and kicked me. An old, weak, grey-haired man. You know, a few blows like that could have killed an ordinary old man. But that wasn't conscious, deliberate execution, was it? Only drunken brutality. Violence in passing. The means to an end. ...You've lost your focus, incidentally. Where are your thoughts about enriching yourself with the money under my mattress, now?

Paul: Mr. Church, I think you think I'm less intelligent than I am.

Mr. Church: [Quietly amused] Really? [Taking the whiskey bottle in his free hand] More whiskey?

Paul:　　　I know you're trying to test me. I could kill people. I could kill her. I could kill you. I could kill you both and then take your money and go. But what good would that do when I'm learning so much from you? ...Do you want me to kill you? You've been pushing me to do it. No-one's that fucking gobbie to a bloke who's kicking him in. Unless he's stupid. You're not a stupid man. So what are you? Suicidal? ...You're going to teach me everything. I can see through you. You want to pass it on. Well I'm the man. I'm your apprentice. ...But ...if I kill *her*, now, I'll shoot her. Then – if you want me to learn - I'll have to torture you. Who else is there? Do you want that? Or is it a quick, clean death you're after? I reckon you're a tough old bastard. If I don't kill you outright, you'll go on for ages before you peg out. Won't you?

Mr. Church:　　　This is a Glock 19 9mm semiautomatic pistol. Perfect for accuracy – hardly any recoil. Fits beautifully in the hand. ...Here. [Walking over to Paul and handing it to him.] Get a feel for the weight. Have a look over it. You need to know your weapon. Handle it. Don't be shy with it.

Paul:　　　[Laughing slightly] Sounds like you're talking about something else.

Mr. Church:　　　[Easy and light in tone] Well, they're not dissimilar. Just make sure you don't get over-excited and let it off before you intend to. [Standing behind Paul, with his hand affectionately resting on Paul's shoulder.] Try picking it up, aiming it. Stand up. That's it. Aim it at the door. Try closing one eye or the other. See what feels right. ...Well, there are two of your weapons. Now the rules. What an assassin needs to remember. Never get emotionally involved. Always view the target in an objective manner. They're not important. They are there so that you can fulfil your work - and to afford you your kicks along the way. You are always superior. You are always alone and godlike, high above these little, little people. [He puts both hands onto Paul's shoulders. Paul relaxes his posture.] Always clean off the weapon before you leave, or take it with you and dispose of it safely. There's another alternative – leave the scene set up to look like a suicide or a murder and suicide. Work out the scene and plant the weapon on the most likely individual.

Paul: It feels so powerful, Mr. Church. Standing here with this gun. It's great. I feel in control. This is what I'm meant to do. I know it. This is totally what my life should be.

Mr. Church: The most important rule, Paul, is to stay aware of where everyone is in the room at all times. Never turn your back on an enemy.

[Mr. Church takes Paul's head in his hands and twists it round, sharply, breaking his neck. Paul slumps down onto his knees and falls forward, awkwardly, onto the floor. Mr. Church picks the gun up out of Paul's hand. He takes it back to the bookcase and lays it beside the stun-gun. He sits back down in his arm-chair.]

Jenny: [Regaining consciousness] Paul?

Mr. Church: You're boyfriend lost his head, I'm afraid. …He won't be much good to you any more. Not that he was, in any case, if we're honest. You have him to thank for your present situation.

Jenny: Paul? …Something hit me?

Mr. Church: That's right. You've been unconscious for some time. Now you're awake, look down. Don't try to get up. You won't be able to.

Jenny: My arms.

Mr. Church: Taped behind your back. Holding you onto that chair.

Jenny: Paul did this?

Mr. Church: Of course, who else could have done?

Jenny: You hit me.

Mr. Church: You're not thinking straight. I'm just a harmless, weak old man.

Jenny: No. I'm right. You hit me.

Mr. Church: Well, you *were* being a very bad girl. Shouting at poor Paul; showing off. Someone had to discipline you. Bring you into line.

Jenny: [Calling, fearfully, to Paul] Paul?

Mr. Church: I did tell you, Paul's not going to be much good to you now. He certainly can't help you. He wouldn't have done, in any case. He wanted to be an assassin. You were to be his first victim. He told me he was going to torture you and then kill you. We'll forget about him, shall we, Jenny? Just concentrate on us.

Jenny: Us, Mr. Church?

Mr. Church: Alasdair.

Jenny: Alasdair?

Mr. Church: You asked me what my Christian name was, remember? I was lying on the ground – your boyfriend had kicked me in the stomach. You came up to me, grabbed my hair and pulled up my head to ask. Was that fun, Jenny? Do you enjoy cruelty?

[Jenny looks at Paul.]

Mr. Church: [Following Jenny's look] He's beginning to annoy me, slumped there. I'll take him for a lie in the bath. Nice and relaxing after the stressful day he's had.

[Mr. Church, showing few indications of vulnerability or unsteadiness, walks across to Paul. He, stands behind him, puts his arms through, under Paul's arms and drags him across the room, past Jenny. Exit stage right.]

Jenny: [Distraught] He's dead. Oh, shit, he's dead! Oh, fuck! Paul! Paul!

[Mr. Church re-enters and goes to sit down on Paul's chair. Jenny observes him silently and in terror.]

Mr. Church: Why don't you scream? You can if you like, it's a good release ...and no-one will hear you: the whole flat is sound-proof.

Jenny: Who *are* you?

Mr. Church: I've already told you: I'm Alasdair. That's my real name, you know. I don't give it to everyone. I used not to give it to anyone, but those days are gone. I'm just an old man in my retirement flat, now.

Jenny: With sound-proof walls and strange doors that lock themselves.

Mr. Church: It's not just the walls that are sound-proofed. Not much point in that. The whole place is sound-proofed – and the windows are bullet-proof.

Jenny: ...That's not true! The whole place isn't sound-proofed! I heard your radio through the door. And I heard you.

Mr. Church: You *are* a clever girl! I'm impressed! And to think so clearly so soon after your boyfriend's death!

Jenny: Cut me free, Mr. Church.

Mr. Church: I haven't told you my true name to be called Mr. Church, have I, Jennifer?

Jenny: I'm Jenny, not Jennifer.

Mr. Church: And I'm Alasdair. I can't cut you free, Jenny.

Jenny: Why not? [She waits for an answer from Alasdair but he resolutely remains mute] Why not, Alasdair?

Mr. Church: Because, my sweet girl. I have so much to teach you first. [He stands up behind Jenny and brushes her cheek with his hand.] You're a prick-tease, Jenny. You came in here and started to flirt with me: an old man, helpless [bends and whispers in her ear], harmless... [Stands back up and walks away from Jenny towards the bookcase] ...but maybe I'm not. [Picking up the stun-gun] Maybe you misjudged. I think that'll be your first lesson. I'll teach you not to underestimate someone based merely on appearances. How safe do you feel, now, Jenny? [Stroking Jenny's cheek, chest, then stomach with the stun-gun.] Trouble with old men is we're not all sweet, kind, defenceless, old men. We just grew older. If a man's a vicious, sadistic young bastard, chances are he'll become a vicious, sadistic old bastard. And we don't all lose interest in *it*, either. [Mr. Church forcefully kisses Jenny.]

[Jenny spits in Mr. Church's face.]

Jenny: Are you trying to scare me?

Mr. Church: [Walking to his radio which he changes to CD] Oh, no. No. I'm succeeding. [*Starting "Steady as She Goes" by The Raconteurs loudly.*] Some mood music, I think. Just in case you scream. Don't want anyone hearing anything they shouldn't, do we? ...Lesson one. Start behind the subject, out of their field of vision. Well back. Move softly. Do everything to disorientate them. [He dims the lights.] Keep them guessing where you are.

[Mr. Church walks slowly and silently towards Jenny who struggles to get off the chair and to get free. He stops behind Jenny.]

Mr. Church: Until you're directly behind them.

[On the words, "Find yourself a girl", Mr. Church starts moving around Jenny. He looks predatory and takes his time, moving the stun-gun up and down her body, picking his place to apply it. He waits for a suitably loud part of the song – the

second "Steady as she goes" - puts the stun-gun to her stomach, under her t-shirt, and pushes the button. Jenny judders and cries out as she feels the volts going through her body. Once the music quietens again, Mr. Church speaks.]

Mr. Church: How did that feel, Jenny? It was good for me. How was it for you? ...When I said little girls get spanked in my house, I might not have been speaking literally. But you have to admit. I didn't let you get away with lying.

[Mr. Church finds another spot he likes and repeats his application of the shock. However, this time, he gives her a series of short, punch-like shocks over the period of the loud music.]

Mr. Church: I'm an aficionado of pain, Jenny. ...Well, every man should have a hobby.

[Mr. Church goes back to his arm-chair, picks up his whiskey glass, fills it from the bottle, puts ice into his glass and drinks. He keeps his glass with him, returns to Jenny and circles her chair. He shocks Jenny a third time.]

Mr. Church: Am I still a harmless, pathetic old man, Jenny? ...Am I? ...Am I gaga? ...Am I helpless, Jenny? ...Defenceless?

[Mr. Church takes another drink of his whiskey then shocks Jenny a fourth time.]

Mr. Church: [Exultantly, over the loud music] I AM GOD!

[Towards the end of the song, there is a sound of banging from above and either side of the flat. At the end of the song, Mr. Church turns the CD player off. Jenny is slumped in her seat. Mr. Church walks back to her, raises her head by her hair and contemplates her face. She has lost consciousness again but suddenly jolts conscious and gasps. Mr. Church forcefully kisses her a second time. This time, Jenny does not react.]

Mr. Church: That's better. Stay quiet. Stay in control. Remember to always think. Plan your strategy. Embrace pain – it makes you stronger. Don't react instinctively. It's never the right decision.

Jenny: I know.

Mr. Church: [In admiration] Oh, you're so strong. So brave. Fuck, you're so intelligent! It's almost a shame it has to end as it does.

Jenny: Does it have to? Why don't you cut me loose? I've learnt your lesson. You've opened my eyes. I'm not the same.

Mr. Church: You'd say anything to convince me, but I can see the truth in your eyes. You were shocked to see death so close. I've inflicted pain on you. Your judgement has improved a little. You can read the situation more sharply, but that should tell you that this isn't over. It can't be – until one of us ends it.

Jenny: How?

Mr. Church: One of us begs for death, Jenny, and the other gives it.

Jenny: It won't be me.

Mr. Church: Are you certain?

Jenny: I've a very strong sense of survival.

Mr. Church: Bet I can take it from you.

Jenny: You're dangerous when you get that tone.

Mr. Church: Am I, Jenny? Why's that?

Jenny: ...Cut me loose, Mr. Church.

Mr. Church: And I thought you were learning, Jenny!

[Mr. Church pulls Jenny from the chair she's sitting on so that she falls face down across the left arm of his arm-chair. He goes to the kitchen, exits stage left and re-enters with a knife. Jenny sees the revolver on top of the bookcase and struggles to get loose. Mr. Church walks back to her, puts the knife between her thighs and cuts the duct tape which holds her upper legs together, leaving her wrists and ankles strapped together.]

Mr. Church: Will this be rape, Jenny? Really? You've been seductive and insolent all the time you've been here. You invited me before I opened the door to you. [He places the knife on the right chair arm in front of Jenny. He stands behind her and grabs both her hips and draws her towards him.]

[Jenny makes a superhuman effort, slides herself forwards, away from Mr. Church and kicks out behind her. Mr. Church tries to move out of her way but is too slow and is kicked. He staggers back and holds onto the back of Jenny's chair. Jenny turns herself over and struggles to get up. She gets the knife in her hands, still behind her back. She crouches down, kneels and cuts the tape between her ankles. She remains there, kneeling with her back to the bookcase and the audience and facing Mr. Church.]

Mr. Church: [Slowly recovering himself.] Oh, Jenny, you've been a very naughty little girl. You're going to pay for that. [He moves towards Jenny, coming in front of the chair.]

Jenny: [Standing up, having pulled her hands out of the tape. Still holding the knife.] I'm not a little girl. I guess you *did* let Paul tape my wrists. You'd have done it much tighter. Apprentice's mistake, I guess.

Mr. Church: *He* was never the apprentice.

Jenny: [Taking the revolver off the bookcase and placing the knife onto the bookcase without taking her eyes off Mr. Church.] So, shall we end it?

Mr. Church: How long were you unconscious?

Jenny: Not as long as you thought I was. How do I do it?

Mr. Church: Aim carefully and calmly. Squeeze the trigger. Aim for the chest with the first shot. Step up to the target, on the floor, and fire into the head with the second shot. To make sure.

Jenny: There is no money in this flat, is there, Mr. Church?

Mr. Church: Alasdair.

Jenny: [Shoots Mr. Church in the chest. With sudden cold command] I'll call you whatever I like, you worthless piece of shit! "One of us begs for death.." So - beg, ...Old Man.

Mr. Church: [Lying on the ground, with his head and shoulders against the chair] The second shot - to the head. Jenny? The second shot.

Jenny: The second shot? Where's best to put that? [She aims downwards at Mr. Church's crotch. Then, she looks up at the front door.] How many bullets are there?

Mr. Church: One, now.

Jenny: How do I open the door?

Mr. Church: You can't. Only my code and fingerprints will open it.

Jenny: Or the second shot?

Mr. Church: Jenny, finish me. You have to. The second shot, Jenny. It's unprofessional behaviour not to.

Jenny: I'm not an assassin. ...And neither are you. What *did* you do, Alasdair?

Mr. Church: The second shot. Please?

Jenny: Whatever you were, you're just a poor, crippled old man, now. The second shot – [She walks up to the key pad by the front door and shoots it. The door opens when she pushes it.]

[Jenny looks as though she is going to go without a backward glance. Then she stops and turns back, keeping her foot in the door to stop it closing. She aims at Alasdair's head with the gun and pulls the trigger. It clicks. She tries a second time but it clicks again. She pauses. She turns to the music system. She presses the CD play button. "Don't Crash the Ambulance" by Mark Knopfler begins to play. Jenny exits through the front door.]

[Alasdair is left, lying on the ground, still leaning against Jenny's chair. He cries out in frustration and pain. Pause. Then he sees the funny side and starts to laugh. He looks around him and sees Paul's glass of whiskey is within reach. He reaches for it and drinks, still laughing to himself.]

Blackout.

"Don't Crash the Ambulance" fades out.

The End.

MEETING THEMSELVES COMING BACK was first performed at four One-Act Play Festivals in 2004, including –

The Bedfordshire Festival, and

The 56th S.W. Herts Drama Festival

At the Bedfordshire Festival, TEAMS 5 Productions, the company which performed the play, picked up nominations for 'Best Dressed Set', 'Adjudicator's Award' (for Best New Play), and 'Best Actor' (for both actors).

At the S.W. Herts Drama Festival, TEAMS 5 Productions were nominated for 'Best Use of Stage', 'Best Director' (for Emma Dinoulis), and 'Best Actor' (for both actors). **MEETING THEMSELVES COMING BACK** also won third place in the category of Best Overall Play.

Simon Nicholas played the role of Prentice

Mark Summers played the role of Rafferty

The stage production benefitted from having a stagehand behind the shelving, hidden by curtains which matched the wings, gradually removing items from the shelves. This helped create physical evidence of Prentice's slow but definite mental unravelling. By the line, "Hang on! ...What is it? ...Whiskey or water?", the whiskey decanter had been replaced with a water jug. By the line, "...Where are your books? Where are your manuscripts? There's nothing! There are no books in the room!" all books had gone from the shelves!

MEETING THEMSELVES COMING BACK
by Emma Dinoulis

Scene One: Prentice's home.

[Prentice is on the patio, smoking a cigarette and dialing a mobile phone. (The actor mimes the cigarette but the mobile phone is real.) Beyond the patio, behind Prentice, the audience can see the living room: neat, spacious, functional. To the side of the main room, stage right, is the doorstep.]

PRENTICE: [On the phone] Mick? Hello, it's Bill. ...Prentice. Look, is Steve in yet? ...No? Good. Can you tell him I'm not coming in this afternoon. ...I know there's loads to do but I need a bit of time off. I haven't been sleeping too well, lately, and... Look... ...I don't care, Mick, I'll take it off as holiday. OK? ...No, fine... Yeah.

[Prentice ends the call and snaps the mobile shut. He puts it in his shirt pocket. He smokes the cigarette, looking thoughtful. He looks around the patio; kicks something on the ground then bends down to pick it up. It is a broken piece of slate. Prentice turns his back to the audience and looks up 'at the roof'.]

PRENTICE: [Throwing slate away] Bloody gales!

[As the slate leaves his hand it grazes it slightly. Prentice inspects his hand then brushes it against his leg and takes his cigarette in that hand. Pause. Prentice drops the cigarette, treads it out then goes through the French windows into the living room.

He goes to a hi-fi system (stage right) and switches it on. A big band number: 'String of Pearls' begins and Prentice sits down in an armchair at the opposite side of the room to listen. A table with a lamp on it stands beside the chair (just left and forward of back centre and between the chair and a sofa). On the table, with the lamp are various ornaments, a notepad, a pen and a glass of whiskey. Prentice sits for a while, eyes closed, with his arms resting on the chair–arms and his head back. After a little while, he sighs and sits forward. He picks up his notepad and turns the leaves. He reads, silently for a few moments, takes a drink and replaces the glass on the table then picks up his pen. The music changes to 'Rain on my Parade' and Prentice looks perturbed. For a while he tries to ignore it then he suddenly throws the notepad at the hi-fi and gets up. Prentice stands for a moment, breathing heavily, then calms himself. He takes a drink of the whiskey and crosses the room. He puts the glass down on the top of the hi-fi and turns the music off. He picks up the notepad, puts it on the chair arm, and returns to the patio. This time, the patio isn't quiet. A magpie rattles somewhere nearby.

Prentice takes out his mobile and switches it on. He checks for messages but there aren't any. He dials a number and waits for a reply. Pause.]

PRENTICE: [Snaps mobile shut again]   God, I hate answerphones!

[Prentice puts the phone back in his pocket and gets out another cigarette. He lights it and puffs away at it for a second or two. He takes out the mobile again; opens it and dials.]

PRENTICE: [Gestures for the message he's listening to to speed up; then, jovially] Alright, yes, hello Annie! You know how much I hate that bloody machine; why don't you answer your phone? Where are you? ...Anyway, I'm at home today if you're getting off early. [Tenderly] ...I don't know what I'm doing really. I thought I'd get some writing done but, I don't know, I just can't be... ...Well, it's not flowing today, anyway. ...Annie, if you're free to come over, I'd love to see you. [Briskly] Let me know! You know where I am! [Pause. Then, reluctantly] ...Bye.

[Prentice stays on the phone for a beat, listening, then ends the call and looks at his phone. He slowly closes it and puts it back in his pocket. Prentice crouches down, then sits on the ground with his back against the French window. He runs his hands through his hair, rubs his eyes then sits quietly, contemplating.

Rafferty appears on the doorstep and there is a knock at the front door. Prentice doesn't look up. Pause. There is another knock. Prentice hears, looks round and gets up. He starts walking into the living room; stops; returns to the patio and throws his cigarette down. He stamps on it as there comes a third knock at the door; blows out a cloud of smoke and walks quickly through the living room, wafting smoke away with his arms.]

PRENTICE: [Answers the door]   Hello?

RAFFERTY: Good afternoon. How are you feeling today?

PRENTICE: What? …Fine, I...

RAFFERTY: I wonder if you'd be interested in buying the New Dark-bulb?

PRENTICE: Dark bulb?

RAFFERTY: [Producing a black-coloured light-bulb]   The New Dark-bulb, TM!

PRENTICE: That's just a light-bulb, painted black.

RAFFERTY: Oh no, it's not.

PRENTICE: What's it supposed to do?

RAFFERTY: If you'd be kind enough to let me in and borrow one of your light fitments, I'll show you.

PRENTICE: [Starting to shut door]   I'm sorry, son, I'm not interested.

RAFFERTY: You're missing a great opportunity! No-ones ever seen this before! Aren't you curious?

PRENTICE: I'm not interested in jokes. [Shuts door]

71

[Rafferty remains on the doorstep – seen by the audience but not Prentice. Prentice walks around the living room for a while then comes back to the front door.]

PRENTICE: [Reopens door] You're still on my doorstep. Why?

RAFFERTY: I think you want to see this.

PRENTICE: Do you?

RAFFERTY: Yes.

[Long pause. Rafferty holds up the dark bulb in front of Prentice]

PRENTICE: Come on then. Come in; show me your little trick and get out.

[Rafferty follows Prentice into the entrance hall]

PRENTICE: [Indicating the hall light]Will this do?

RAFFERTY: A table lamp would be easier.   I'll need something to stand on to get to this fitting.   ...A stepladder or something.

PRENTICE: [Suspiciously]   Got any ID on you?

RAFFERTY: [Shows badge]   I'm not a thief, you know! I'm a salesman. I'm here to offer you something amazing.

PRENTICE: [Shaking his head]   Come on then. [He leads the way into the living room]

RAFFERTY: [Walks to table-lamp]   OK to use this one?

[Prentice nods and laughs, incredulously. Rafferty takes the lamp shade off and unscrews the bulb from the fitting. He puts the dark bulb into the fitting and presses the switch. Nothing happens.]

PRENTICE: Oh, very impressive! Come on. You've wasted my time quite enough. Out you go!

RAFFERTY: It's not switched on at the wall.

[Prentice goes to the wall and looks. He crouches down and switches on the power.

BLACKOUT.

There is a crash and Prentice exclaims]

PRENTICE: What the....?

RAFFERTY: It's the Dark-bulb.

PRENTICE: It's pitch black!

RAFFERTY: Dark – like the night.

PRENTICE: It's two o'clock in the afternoon!

RAFFERTY: Switch it off again at the mains.

PRENTICE: I can't find the switch.

[The lights come back on. Rafferty is standing with the lamp in his hand. He holds it like a club – the dark-bulb at the top. Prentice is lying on his stomach, on the floor. The table is knocked over and the ornaments are scattered around Prentice.]

PRENTICE: What the hell was that?

RAFFERTY: The New Dark-bulb, TM.

PRENTICE: Liar! …It must have been an eclipse.

RAFFERTY: No eclipse. I told you – it's the Dark-bulb.

PRENTICE: The daylight went! You can't switch off the sun!

RAFFERTY: I can show you again, if you like?

PRENTICE: No!

RAFFERTY: You won't believe me if I don't. You'll think it was a scam! Let me show you again?

PRENTICE: No! No! I don't want you to! Just get out!

RAFFERTY: There's blood on your head.

PRENTICE: The daylight went!

RAFFERTY: Did you hit your head on the table?

PRENTICE: It's impossible! …What did you do?

RAFFERTY: Hold still. Don't get up. I'll show you again.

[BLACKOUT]

PRENTICE: What is it?

RAFFERTY: The New Dark-bulb, TM.

PRENTICE: The 'new' dark-bulb?

74

RAFFERTY: There have been others.

PRENTICE: Switch it off.

RAFFERTY: Where are you?

PRENTICE: Why?

RAFFERTY: I want you to switch it off, or you won't believe
it's the dark bulb doing it.

PRENTICE: Don't be a little bastard! Switch it off!

RAFFERTY: Mr Prentice…

PRENTICE: OK, I'm here. Where is it? Where's the switch?
Ow, fuck, you're standing on my arm!

[Lights up. Prentice is on his back. He is holding the lamp on
his chest. Rafferty is standing next to him, one foot on
Prentice's arm.]

PRENTICE: You're on my arm! Get off!

RAFFERTY: **[Not moving his foot]**   I'm sorry, Mr Prentice.

PRENTICE: Don't be sorry, just get off!

RAFFERTY: **[Unscrews Dark-Bulb & walks a few paces**
(stage left) with it.]   Thank you.

PRENTICE: How do you know my name?

RAFFERTY: You must have told me it.

PRENTICE: I didn't!

RAFFERTY: I was told to come here. They thought you'd be
interested.

PRENTICE: Who did?

RAFFERTY: The manufacturers.

PRENTICE: Why would I want one?

RAFFERTY: Maybe it would be useful for your work? What do you do? ...Are you a murderer?

PRENTICE: Am I a murderer? No! ...Of course I'm not.

RAFFERTY: How can you be so sure?

PRENTICE: What are you talking about?

RAFFERTY: How would you know?

PRENTICE: I don't think it's something I could overlook. **[Tense laugh]**

RAFFERTY: **[Taking pills out of his pocket and approaching Prentice]** Get up, Mr. Prentice. Do you want me to help you?

PRENTICE: Stay away from me! **[Sitting up but remaining on the ground]** ...I can get up on my own.

RAFFERTY: **[Showing pills]** Have you tried these before?

PRENTICE: What are they?

RAFFERTY: Medicine.

PRENTICE: You're a drug dealer?

RAFFERTY: **[Laughing]**   That's right! I'm a drug-dealer!

PRENTICE: I thought you were a salesman.

RAFFERTY: I never told you that - that's what you said.

PRENTICE: The Dark-Bulb... You wanted to sell that to me – to use it to...

RAFFERTY: I think you'd better take these.

PRENTICE: What are they?

RAFFERTY: They'll make you feel better. ...You can take them on their own or with that water. **[He gestures to the glass on top of the hi-fi]**

PRENTICE: Water? What water? That's whiskey.

RAFFERTY: There's blood on your head, Mr Prentice.

PRENTICE: I'm not a murderer. That's whiskey!

RAFFERTY: Try drinking some.

PRENTICE: Why are you trying to trick me? You've done nothing else since I let you in! ...I want you to leave; and you can take your drugs and your Dark-Bulbs and your crazy suggestions with you!

RAFFERTY: I'm sorry, Mr Prentice, but I'm not supposed to leave. ...And I wouldn't want to leave you like this, anyway. You're obviously upset, and you've hurt yourself. Let me help you up.

[Rafferty goes towards Prentice and tries to support him by putting his arm under Prentice's and holding him round his back.]

PRENTICE: **[Flinches and backs away]** You might stab me! ...Show me what you've got in your hands.

RAFFERTY: **[Shows his hands]** Empty.

[Rafferty helps Prentice up and into the arm-chair.]

RAFFERTY: Let me get you a drink.

PRENTICE: [Nods] Thanks!

[Prentice watches as Rafferty walks over to the Hi-fi, picks up
the glass and takes a decanter from the sideboard.]

PRENTICE: Hang on! …What is it? …Whiskey or water?

RAFFERTY: W… …You tell me!

PRENTICE: Whiskey.

RAFFERTY: OK, it's whiskey. [Pours the drink & hands
Prentice the glass]

PRENTICE: [Takes it then pauses]   You might have spiked
it.

RAFFERTY: I give you my word I haven't.

PRENTICE: The word of a drug dealer?   [Drinks]
…It's water!

RAFFERTY: I told you it was!

PRENTICE: What have you done to it? What have you done
to me? [Gets up from the chair. Throws the glass aside and
seizes Rafferty] You've drugged me! You little bastard! You
slipped it in my drink. …No wonder I believed the "Dark-Bulb"!
There's no such thing! …It made the sunshine disappear! It
switched the sun off! …There's no such thing!

RAFFERTY: You had it in your hands! You controlled it!

PRENTICE: Are you trying to tell me that it's real?

RAFFERTY: Why don't you try it again?

PRENTICE: Where is it?

RAFFERTY: Here.

PRENTICE: Give it to me. Sit down. …In the armchair. Go on - Sit!

[Rafferty sits. Prentice picks up the lamp and sits down on the sofa, looking at the Dark-Bulb.]

RAFFERTY: Don't you remember the murders?

PRENTICE: [Still engrossed] Murders? Back on that again? [Screws Dark-Bulb into fitting]

RAFFERTY: Why don't you turn the Dark-Bulb on again? …It might help you see.

PRENTICE: …What? …You're a sick boy! I don't know what you're doing here and I know you shouldn't be being sent around as a travelling salesman!

RAFFERTY: Do you see the Devil in the dark?

PRENTICE: Do I what?

RAFFERTY: Turn on the Dark-Bulb, Prentice: switch off the sun. Look into the mirror! Do you see your eyes glinting like blood in the moonlight? Do you see the killer? Do you meet yourself coming back?

PRENTICE: I'm going to call the police.

RAFFERTY: You haven't got a phone – you're not allowed one.

PRENTICE: [Putting the lamp down on the sofa next to him] I've got a mobile, here, in my pocket. [Reaches into his shirt pocket but there isn't anything in it] Shit! [Looks around on the floor for where the mobile might have fallen. He

scrabbles about on his hands and knees. He stops and turns to kneel in front of Rafferty in the armchair| Look, mate, what's you're name?

RAFFERTY: What's my name? ...Don't you know me?

PRENTICE: Please, son, come on. Just tell me what to call you.

RAFFERTY: Rafferty.

PRENTICE: Rafferty. Tell me, why do you think I'm a murderer?

RAFFERTY: Mr. Prentice, I...

PRENTICE: |**Laughing|** My notepad! ...My writing? ...Have you been in here - sneaking about - and found my writing? Oh, Rafferty! |**Relieved|**, it's not real, you silly boy!

RAFFERTY: I'm not a boy, Mr. Prentice.

PRENTICE: Of course you're not, Rafferty, I'm sorry. ...Listen, Rafferty, I'm a writer. ...I write about horrific things – but I've never **done** them. Listen to me, Rafferty - I'm interested in the mind: the human psyche. I believe that everyone has terrible things in them – instincts for violence, brutality, cruelty. Of course, there are wonderful things in us too, Rafferty – kindness, empathy, love – but I think that it's dangerous not to acknowledge the bad things! If you repress them, that's when they're strongest – when you ignore the fact that they're there. ...I don't ignore them. I let the waking nightmares come. I see terrifying things in here |**taps his head|**, but I don't block them out. I don't dam it up. I let it flow. ...I **write** them! I use them all! I pour them out on paper! ...Can you imagine – if I let these terrible thoughts out in actions –

80

if I took the destructive way instead of the creative? But I don't, Rafferty! I pour it out in ink. You can't hurt people with pen and ink, Rafferty!

RAFFERTY: Mr. Prentice, you're not a writer...

PRENTICE: No, well, I haven't had much luck yet. I've got a nine to five job (I've got to live)... ...But I **do** write - I write in my own time.

RAFFERTY: You don't, Mr. Prentice! You don't write! ...Where are your books? Where are your manuscripts? There's nothing! There are no books in the room!

PRENTICE: Calm down, Rafferty! You're getting hysterical! ...My notepad! I'll show you my notepad – I was reading it just before you came in.

RAFFERTY: **[Finding the notepad]**   This is your notepad. **[displaying the pages to Prentice]** There's no writing in it! Every page is blank!

PRENTICE: ...What? No! Let me see that. **[Snatches it from Rafferty]** It's not mine. This isn't mine. It can't be. ...Why are you doing this, Rafferty? What are you doing all this for?

RAFFERTY: Turn on the Dark-Bulb, Mr. Prentice. Go on. Turn it on. Doesn't the sunshine dazzle your mind? No wonder you can't think straight with all this sun in your eyes! Switch off the sun, Mr. Prentice. Then you can make the journey.

PRENTICE: What journey?

RAFFERTY: Down the spiral staircase – into the core of the Earth.

PRENTICE: Down the spiral staircase?

RAFFERTY: Into the core of your self.

PRENTICE: Rafferty...

RAFFERTY: [Suddenly]   Or should we change the
subject?

PRENTICE: I think... Rafferty... ...Would you like a drink?
Do you mind if I put some music on? Quiet, calming music, I
mean.

RAFFERTY: That sounds very nice, thank you. ...I'd like
water.

**[Prentice goes to the hi-fi and puts on 'Aesa's Death' from 'Peer
Gynt'. He starts pouring a glass of water from the whiskey
decanter.]**

RAFFERTY: [Laughs]   Do you mind if we change this?

PRENTICE: [Jabs at the stop button] No, of course not.
Sorry! ...Why?

RAFFERTY: Well, I can never take it seriously. It reminds me
of the theme tune to "Postman Pat".

PRENTICE: "Postman Pat"?

RAFFERTY: Yes, "Postman Pat". ...Look, I'll show you what
I mean. I'll sing the theme tune to "Postman Pat" then, on my
signal, you start that up again! OK?

PRENTICE: Alright... **[Puts down the whiskey decanter
and prepares the CD player]**

RAFFERTY: [Sings] "Postman Pat, Postman Pat, Postman Pat
and his black and white cat". **[Signals to Prentice to start the CD,**

then sings with the dirge] "Post-man Pa-at, Post-man Pa-at, Post-man Pat and his black and white ca-at". **[Signals for Prentice to stop the CD]** See what I mean? I just can't help thinking of it as a dirge for Postman Pat!

PRENTICE: Let me get you that water. **[Gives glass to Rafferty]**

RAFFERTY: Thanks.

PRENTICE: **[Sitting down on the sofa and picking up the lamp again]**   I hope you realise you've ruined that piece of music for me, now!

RAFFERTY: Sorry. Don't let me stop you playing music. …If it makes you feel better.

PRENTICE: It's alright; I don't mind.

RAFFERTY: No, please, go on. Play something else.

PRENTICE: I don't want music on, now, I don't feel like it.

RAFFERTY: I thought it calmed you down.

PRENTICE: I thought it might calm **you** down!

RAFFERTY: Me? I'm perfectly calm.

PRENTICE: Well, we don't need music, then.

RAFFERTY: Play something else.

PRENTICE: No.

RAFFERTY: Go on. I want you to.

PRENTICE: Alright, alright! …Anything for a peaceful life!

[Prentice goes to the hi-fi and puts on a CD of Noel Coward songs (Coward singing), starting with '20th Century Blues'.]

RAFFERTY: What's this?

PRENTICE: Noel Coward. …Like it?

RAFFERTY: It's not very …positive.

PRENTICE: The next one will be.

RAFFERTY: You don't want to depress yourself again.

PRENTICE: When was I depressed?

RAFFERTY: When I came in.

PRENTICE: I wasn't depressed.

RAFFERTY: You were low.

PRENTICE: How do **you** know?

RAFFERTY: I can tell.

PRENTICE: **You** might have been low – **I** wasn't.

RAFFERTY: You seemed pensive.

PRENTICE: I was thinking.

RAFFERTY: What were you thinking about?

PRENTICE: I was trying to write.

RAFFERTY: **[Slight alarm]**   Were you?

PRENTICE: Yes.

RAFFERTY: **[Suspicious]**   What about?

[PAUSE]

RAFFERTY: What about?

PRENTICE: I think I **will** change this music: you're right, it's
not very upbeat.

RAFFERTY: Where's the Dark-Bulb, Mr. Prentice?

PRENTICE: I'm not going to turn it on again. Don't think you can trick me into it!

RAFFERTY: No; I just want it back.

PRENTICE: You want it?

RAFFERTY: It's a very valuable prototype. I have to take it back to the manufacturers undamaged.

PRENTICE: You gave it to me.

RAFFERTY: I showed it to you - now I need it back! …Please.

PRENTICE: **[Picks up the lamp from the sofa and sits, looking into the Dark-Bulb]**   What if I don't want to give it back?

RAFFERTY: You have to give it back. You don't have a choice.

PRENTICE: Who's going to take it back from me, Rafferty? Are you? I'm a lot stronger than you. I could make mincemeat out of you. I can chew you up and spit you out. I can break you.

RAFFERTY: I have to take it back to the manufacturers undamaged.

PRENTICE: Who's going to take **you** back undamaged?

RAFFERTY: Mr. Prentice, calm down!

PRENTICE: No, Rafferty, I won't calm down! You come in here to show me this trick – this bauble; you spike my drink; you tread on me; you use my house as your own; you accuse me of rape and torture; you hound me; you hunt me down; you lie to me; you crush my dreams; you worry me; you weary me… …I'm so tired!

RAFFERTY: I was wrong to try and take it away, Mr. Prentice. I'm sorry. You need it. Turn it on again, Mr. Prentice; there's nothing to fear and everything to gain.

[Prentice switches on the Dark-Bulb. BLACKOUT]

PRENTICE: …I wasn't trying to write. I'd given up. I was calling my friend… Annie.

RAFFERTY: **[Alarm]** You were what?

PRENTICE: She's a lovely woman. Beautiful – intelligent – she understands me. I really believe she loves me…

RAFFERTY: You were trying to ring Annie?

PRENTICE: She has lovely golden hair…

RAFFERTY: Mr. Prentice?

PRENTICE: …And sea-blue eyes…

RAFFERTY: Annie?

PRENTICE: …They sparkle when she laughs! I love it when I can make her laugh…

RAFFERTY: Listen to me, Mr. Prentice!

PRENTICE: …And a body to die for!

RAFFERTY: A body to kill for?

PRENTICE: What?

RAFFERTY: Are you trying to tell me you spoke to Annie?

PRENTICE: No, I couldn't speak to her. I couldn't get through. It was just her sodding answerphone.

RAFFERTY: It always will be, Mr. Prentice. …It'll always be the answerphone. You can't speak to Annie. She'll never answer you.

PRENTICE: Why not?

[LIGHTS BACK ON]

PRENTICE: What are you talking about?

RAFFERTY: Mr. Prentice, I think I **will** take that back, now. **[holds out his hand for the Dark-Bulb]**

PRENTICE: No you won't. Tell me why you think Annie won't talk to me. …You don't even know her.

RAFFERTY: No, I don't. I'm sorry. I shouldn't have said anything.

PRENTICE: Rafferty, why won't Annie speak to me? I want to know.

RAFFERTY: Listen to the music, Mr. Prentice. …this is a fun one, isn't it!

PRENTICE: Don't patronise me, you little tosser! Sod the music! …Turn it off. Go on! Go and turn it off! I want to talk to you properly …with no distractions.

[Rafferty goes to the hi-fi and switches off the music]

PRENTICE: You seem to know your way around my house awfully well! What are you? A little thief?

RAFFERTY: Mr. Prentice…

PRENTICE: Come here. Stand here – in front of me.

RAFFERTY: Mr. Prentice, I think I should go.

PRENTICE: No you don't.

RAFFERTY: I won't be long – I'll come back.

PRENTICE: You're not going anywhere! You should have left ages ago but you refused to go...

[Rafferty puts his hand on Prentice's shoulder]

PRENTICE: Don't manhandle me! ...You should never really have come here, should you? But you did. What are you doing here?

RAFFERTY: I work here.

PRENTICE: In my house?

RAFFERTY: This isn't your house, it's a ...hospital. ...You're not well, Mr. Prentice. I was sent to you by the Devil. He told me to sew up your eyes and put blood in your ears so that you wouldn't get confused anymore...

PRENTICE: What?

RAFFERTY: The Devil – he gave me the new Dark-Bulb TM, to calm you down and help you see. Turn it on again, Mr. Prentice.

PRENTICE: No I won't! I don't want to be in the dark with you - you're loopy!

RAFFERTY: Turn it on or I'll do it!

[Both Rafferty and Prentice make a dive for the lamp (on the sofa). Rafferty grabs it and holds it away from Prentice, his thumb on the switch]

PRENTICE: Rafferty, Rafferty give me that! Rafferty, listen to me, son, it's not safe!

[BLACKOUT]

PRENTICE: Oh, Rafferty... You shouldn't have done that!
RAFFERTY: Tell me about her, Prentice. Tell me about Annie. Tell me about the last time you saw her.
PRENTICE: Rafferty. You don't know what you're doing. Turn the Dark-Bulb off! Bring the sun back, Prentice!
RAFFERTY: Prentice? ...I'm Rafferty! You're Prentice, Mr. Prentice.
PRENTICE: Bring the sunlight back, Prentice! Bring it back! I'm warning you!
RAFFERTY: Tell me about Annie!
PRENTICE: No!
RAFFERTY: Tell me about her or I'll never let the sun back! I'll leave you in the dark – with the pain.
PRENTICE: No.
RAFFERTY: Describe her to me, as you saw her last. What was she wearing? ...What colour was she wearing?

[A very tight, blue shaft of light starts to come up slowly on Prentice from this point, dimly revealing him, in a foetal position on the sofa. Prentice's body language expands as his speech continues. The light never gets higher than half way to full on.]

PRENTICE: Blue. Midnight blue – a satin trouser suit… and a grey silk top. It – felt – so… And her skin was silk as well… so beautiful… so pale – like porcelain.

RAFFERTY: Where were you?

PRENTICE: Her place. …I didn't really like it. She had a strip light and it kept cutting out. Drove me nuts! Flashing on and off… I offered to fix it but she said it didn't bother her.

RAFFERTY: But it bothered you.

PRENTICE: Drove me nuts! …Of course, when we… got down to it… I didn't notice whether it was on or off or what was happening.

RAFFERTY: Intense.

PRENTICE: [Laughs]   Bloody hell, yeah! …It was so – amazing! Just looking at her, then running my hands down her smooth, cool body. I couldn't believe I was doing it. I caught myself holding my breath… [Laughs] Isn't that crazy! It was like reverence – I couldn't believe I was allowed to touch her, somehow… But nothing could have stopped me then! When that incredible, suspended moment finally ended, I was so fired up! I could feel my own breath coming back at me, warm, off her shoulder and her neck. I just grabbed her! I felt …invincible! So much power – adrenalin – pumping through me! What a surge!

RAFFERTY: And then?

PRENTICE: [Sardonic] And then? [Distraught] …And then the nightmares came again. I couldn't believe it! "Why now?", I thought. It was so …unfair. It was the last thing I wanted – for the nightmares to taint my time with her. She was so pure: so untouched. How cruel to take that away from me! She was my haven. A calm embrace protecting me from the mad panic of life! But, suddenly, I saw she was part of it all. All the crushing coldness of the world. Impersonal. Uncaring. I looked into her eyes and they were dead. There was no love in them for me. I felt so much for her – for me, this was transcendent – for her it was just mechanical! The whore! I wanted to beat her brains out – tear out her stone heart and break it in front of her. …Such pain! I feel such pain!

[LIGHTS BACK UP.]

[Prentice is sitting on the sofa. Rafferty places the lamp on the table]

RAFFERTY: Mr. Prentice, you have to stop this. You have to!

PRENTICE: You started it. It's your fault. You should never have demanded it. You should never have pushed me.

RAFFERTY: Mr. Prentice, I'm going to get you help.

PRENTICE: Help? Help for me? There's no help for me. There's no hope. None at all. …I killed her. Didn't I?

RAFFERTY: Yes.

PRENTICE: You knew? …And you made me re-live it. Cruel. Cruel!

RAFFERTY: Mr. Prentice, if anything I said has set you thinking about it, I'm truly sorry, I never meant to...

PRENTICE: You liar.

RAFFERTY: [Walking to the front door and opening it] I'll get others.

[Prentice follows Rafferty and shuts the door, trapping him. Rafferty turns round to look at Prentice, who grabs his throat with one hand and pushes him against the wall]

PRENTICE: You're a liar. ...Or a madman. Can you only get enjoyment out of other people's pain? You're dirt! You don't deserve to live.

[Rafferty kicks Prentice, wrestles him off and runs for the French windows. Rafferty struggles with the sliding door and Prentice walks into the room, behind him. Prentice picks up the lamp in his right hand and, with his left, grabs Rafferty's arm as Rafferty is getting through the French window, onto the patio.]

PRENTICE: Where are you going to run to now?

RAFFERTY: Mr. Prentice... Please!

PRENTICE: I've got the Dark-Bulb now. I'm in control. How are you going to hide from me? I control the darkness – I'm master over the sun.

[BLACKOUT]

RAFFERTY: Mr. Prentice, please listen to me – I'm telling you the truth. I'm a nurse. I'm a nurse - I've been helping you: visiting you for months. Look at my uniform, Mr. Prentice. Look at my face. Don't you recognise me?

PRENTICE: Oh, yes. I recognise you. …I don't think you recognise yourself, though. Come back into the living-room. Come on. Come back in here. Let me show you your reflection in the mirror. Let's both look. Who do you think we'll see? Shall we look, Prentice? Shall we meet ourselves coming back? We'll see the real us soon.

[Sounds of a struggle and stabbing]

RAFFERTY: Mr. Prentice, no! …Please! …Help! …*Dad!*

[An alarm goes off and a blue light starts flashing. It is still very dark but we can just see that it is the living-room and pick out Prentice, standing over Rafferty with the jagged piece of slate in his hand. Rafferty is wearing a uniform and there are stab-wounds to his torso. Mark Knopfler's 'Marbletown' begins to play. Fade to blackout with music still playing.]

THE END

WITHIN DOORS

WITHIN DOORS was specifically written with the actors in mind and was written to be an enjoyable play for them to perform. The role of Jean (or "Mum") should be particularly enjoyable for a middle-aged actress as it gives her the chance to play the most powerful and dominant character!

Dave (or "Dad") is a quietly menacing character, cowed by Jean but more than a match for the younger characters.

And then there's the question of which of the young characters, Andy or Susie, is actually the enemy within!

WITHIN DOORS

by Emma Dinoulis

<u>Characters:</u>

Jean	-	Woman, 50 – 60
Dave	-	Man, 49-60
Andy	-	Man, 20-30
Susie	-	Woman, 20-30

<u>Scene:</u>

A Kitchen / Diner. A long dining table with five or six chairs around it. A sideboard with two stools by it. A television mounted on one wall and a rocking chair in the corner. JEAN is sitting in the rocking chair, reading a newspaper. DAVE is at the cooker, making a cooked breakfast. ANDY and SUSIE are sitting on stools, playing cards across the sideboard. There are empty mugs on the table and the sideboard and the remote control for the television is by the cooker.

DAVE: Anyone want *two* eggs?

JEAN: [Looking at her watch] Remote.

DAVE: [Handing JEAN the remote] What did your last slave die of?

JEAN: Stupidity!

JEAN turns on the television. She flicks through the channels impatiently. ANDY and SUSIE look up at the screen.

JEAN: How do you get teletext on this thing?

ANDY: Press the teletext button.

JEAN gives ANDY a withering look and presses the button.
Loud, quiz-show music starts playing.

JEAN: Bloody thing! Where's the mute?

ANDY: **[Jumps down from his stool and crosses to JEAN]** Let
me see?

JEAN gives ANDY the remote

ANDY: **[Mutes the sound]** Which page is it on?

JEAN: How should I know? Can't you just flick through
them?

ANDY: I need to know where to start.

SUSIE: No you don't. Just check all of them.

DAVE: Who wants *two* eggs?

ANDY: **[Raises his hand]** Yeah. **[Presses more buttons]** There
you go.

ALL watch the screen for a few moments. DAVE forgets to
watch the frying pan for a while until the fat spits and burns his
hand slightly. He winces and his attention returns to the
cooking.

ANDY: Nothing!

SUSIE: I told you there wouldn't be anything yet.

JEAN: You always know everything, don't you!

SUSIE: Sorry! ...I just think it's a bit soon.

ANDY and DAVE both look tense. They glance at SUSIE then turn to look at JEAN.

JEAN: **[Fixes SUSIE with a stare. PAUSE. She suddenly breaks off, takes the remote back from ANDY and switches the television off. Putting the remote down at the side of her rocking chair]** Fair enough. We'll look again later. **[Returning to her newspaper]** How's breakfast coming on?

DAVE: It's all here. What do you want?

JEAN: I'll have a bit of everything.

DAVE: Coffee?

JEAN: Tea.

DAVE takes a plate out of the oven and puts a sausage, egg, bacon, beans, a tomato and a piece of fried bread on it. He places it at the head of the table and breaks another egg into the frying pan.

SUSIE: **[To ANDY]** Aren't you going to finish this hand?

ANDY: **[Returning to the sideboard]** What's the point? You're cheating!

SUSIE: **[Laughs]** Who is?

ANDY: [Laughs] You are, you little cheat! You've got cards hidden everywhere – up both sleeves, in your pockets, down your knickers!

SUSIE: Have not!

ANDY: I know you have.

SUSIE: Prove it!

ANDY: [Grabs SUSIE and starts fishing in her clothing, scattering cards everywhere] Let's look down here, shall we?

SUSIE screams and laughs. DAVE watches, amused.

JEAN: [Puts down the paper and sighs] Cut that out, you two! You'll put me off my breakfast!

JEAN gets up from the rocking chair, straightens her newspaper and takes her seat at the head of the table, placing her paper on the table by her. SUSIE and ANDY takes seats to the left and right of her, respectively, and DAVE places JEAN's tea on the table.

ANDY: [To JEAN] How long do you think it'll be before we know, Mum?

JEAN: [Nodding at SUSIE] Why don't you ask the 'Fount of Wisdom', here?

DAVE places breakfasts in front of ANDY and SUSIE.

SUSIE: I'm sorry, Jean, I didn't...

JEAN: [Corrects] Mum!

SUSIE: Mum. I'm sorry, I was just trying to use a bit of common sense. I don't think we will know anything for a while.

JEAN: [Sounding dangerous] 'Common sense'? What do you think I use?

SUSIE: Well, I think...

DAVE: [Cutting in] I think you should take over cooking the last breakfast, Susie!

SUSIE: What? ...But, I...

DAVE: [Pulling SUSIE's chair out with her on it, then undoing his apron and offering it to her] Here, you'll need this!

SUSIE: I thought this was mine!

DAVE: Yeah, well it's mine now – get up and make your own! You've already got sausages and beans on a plate in the oven. [Heavy sarcasm] You can fry an egg, can you?

SUSIE reluctantly rises from her seat, takes the apron and ties it round her. DAVE sits in her place, takes a bite of the fried bread and smiles at her.

DAVE: Mmmmm...

SUSIE turns away and starts preparing her breakfast. She cracks an egg into the frying pan.

ANDY: [To SUSIE] Make us a cup of tea while you're there.

SUSIE: Make your own, you cheeky so-and-so!

ANDY rises from his chair and joins SUSIE by the cooker. He switches on the kettle and gets out a teabag.

JEAN: Get me a cup, too! This one's stone cold!

DAVE: I'll have a coffee.

ANDY takes JEAN's mug from the table and makes the drinks. He takes drinks to JEAN and DAVE and sits back down with his own drink during the next few lines.

SUSIE: It's funny we haven't heard anything from Rob Clark!

JEAN: It's not! ...We never hear from Rob until after five o'clock.

SUSIE: Why not?

JEAN: He works at a bookshop until then.

SUSIE: What? Rob works at a bookshop?

JEAN: He owns it.

SUSIE: A bookies?

JEAN: **[Aggressively]** Did I say 'a bookies'?

DAVE: **[Scornfully, to SUSIE]** No. A bookshop.

ANDY: Well, that's not the point, is it? It doesn't matter where he works. It just means we won't hear from him before five.

DAVE: Correct.

SUSIE: So, unless it does come up on teletext, we've got – what? – nine hours to wait?

DAVE: Probably.

SUSIE: Do we all have to wait together, here?

JEAN: Got somewhere else you desperately want to be?

SUSIE: Well, no, but...

JEAN: Good! Get your breakfast, sit down and shut up! ...I've been over this a hundred times – we're all going to stay here until we've heard and know for certain.

SUSIE: But...

DAVE: [Suddenly stands up, spins round and comes close up behind SUSIE. Whispers aggressively] Shut up! Can't you keep your mouth shut, you little idiot? ...Sit down! [He takes her shoulder, turns her round and pushes her towards the table, indicating the chair next to ANDY's]

SUSIE: [Turning back, sheepishly] My breakfast?

DAVE: [Pause] ...I'll bring it over to you.

SUSIE walks, nervously, round the back of JEAN's chair and takes her place downstage of ANDY.

ANDY: [Whispers, agreeably] Naughty girl! Always getting into trouble!

JEAN: [To ANDY] And you can can it, too!

ANDY raises his hands in a sign of appeasement and returns to his breakfast. DAVE finishes SUSIE's breakfast and places it in front of her before sitting down again, himself.

JEAN: [To DAVE] Got a cigarette?

DAVE: No. I'm out.

JEAN: I hope you're kidding!

DAVE: I'm sorry, I really don't have any left. ...I had my last one at Rob's and, we came back here in such a rush, I didn't have a chance to buy any more.

JEAN: Shit! ...Either of you two smoke?

ANDY and SUSIE look at one another and smile

ANDY & SUSIE: [Together] No, Mum!

JEAN: Come on, cut out the funny stuff! Either of you have any fags?

ANDY and SUSIE shake their heads

JEAN: Shit! ...Nine hours of this and we've got no cigarettes?

SUSIE: I could nip round the corner for some!

JEAN: You're nipping nowhere! I told you! We all stay together until we hear! [To DAVE] Get me a coffee!

DAVE: You're drinking tea! [He takes JEAN's cup] ...And you haven't touched it!

JEAN: [Looks angry, then softens] Come on, Dad! Let's have that coffee!

DAVE: [Catching her lighter mood] OK, Mum! One lump or two?

JEAN: Black – no sugar. Thanks!

DAVE: [As though starting an old routine] What a couple of kids we have here, eh, Mum? Both happy enough to sit about and watch their old Dad slave away over a hot stove!

ANDY: [Corrects] Over a hot kettle! ...I've just made the drinks!

DAVE: Never a thought for anyone but themselves!

JEAN: [Picking up her newspaper again] And that one, [nodding at SUSIE] always right, no matter what the subject. What a clever cloggs! [Starts reading the newspaper]

SUSIE: Has everyone finished? Shall we wash up?

DAVE: [Passing JEAN her coffee – mock surprise] Ooooh! I think we've shamed them into washing up, Mother!

SUSIE and ANDY collect up plates and empty mugs. DAVE wanders over to the sideboard and starts collecting the playing cards together. JEAN gets up and moves back to her rocking chair. SUSIE and ANDY wash up.

JEAN: [Still reading her newspaper and rocking in her chair] "Spurned wife shoots love rival"... ...Stupid bitch!

DAVE: What? I'd have thought you'd approve of that?

JEAN: She shot her in broad daylight - in front of witnesses! She must have been unhinged! Why go to prison for a dirty little slut like that? ...Anyway, I'd have had the two-timing husband bumped off, personally! …Preferably, as painfully and slowly as possible!

DAVE: Nice.

SUSIE: I don't think anyone would be stupid enough to cross you, Mum!

DAVE: Don't you? **[Stoops down to pick up cards from the floor]**

JEAN: What's that supposed to mean?

ANDY: [Quickly] Anything else of interest?

JEAN: **[To DAVE]** What did you mean?

DAVE: Nothing… nothing… Go back to your rag! **[Stays low]**

JEAN: **[Putting down the paper and getting up]** Who would cross me? You? You spineless creep?

DAVE: Look, there's no need for that!

JEAN: **[Advancing across the room towards him]** Would you?

DAVE: No! No, not me!

JEAN: **[Stopping at the head of the table]** Who, then?

DAVE half turns in SUSIE's direction

JEAN: Not Susie? Our resident know-it-all? **[Turning on SUSIE]**

SUSIE: I wouldn't cross you, Mum! Of course I wouldn't! You didn't mean that, did you, Dad?

DAVE: 'Course not! 'Course I didn't, Mum! Why don't you settle down with your paper again?

JEAN: I'm not to be messed around with!

ANDY: [picking up JEAN's newspaper] This isn't today's. Do you want me to get it? I've seen it somewhere. In the front room?

JEAN: It's in the hall, somewhere. Yes. [Sitting down in the rocker] Thanks! I'd like it.

ANDY turns to go out of the room (stage right)

JEAN: [Stopping ANDY with her voice] Andy! Don't go in the front room! I want us all to keep to the back of the house, OK?

ANDY: [Under his breath] It's going to be a long nine hours!

JEAN: What?

ANDY: Nothing! [Exits]

SUSIE: Mum? You don't believe I'd cross you, do you?

ANDY re-enters and gives JEAN the new newspaper

JEAN: [As ANDY starts to walk away from her] Hold on, Andy! [She rolls up the old paper] You can put this one in the bin.

ANDY returns to JEAN and leans down to her to take it.
JEANS smacks ANDY round the ear with the rolled-up paper

JEAN: Don't whisper behind people's backs – it's rude! [Thrusts the paper at him to take] Here!

ANDY takes the old paper and puts it in the bin then he takes the hitherto unused seat at the table, nursing his ear. JEAN opens today's newspaper and reads in silence.

SUSIE: Mum?

SUSIE leaves the sink and moves closer to JEANS's rocking chair. DAVE stands in front of the side-board, shuffling the cards he's been picking up.

DAVE: [Hisses across the room at SUSIE] Leave her alone! Come here!

SUSIE walks away from JEAN, past ANDY to meet DAVE by the sideboard

DAVE: What the hell do you think you're playing at? Why do you keep pushing her, like that? Didn't you see how worked up she was?
SUSIE: Well, I just thought…
DAVE: You're not thinking at all! …What did you think?
SUSIE: I just don't want her thinking I'm against her!
DAVE: And you think the more you go on about it the less she'll think that way, do you?
SUSIE: I just want the situation clarified.
DAVE: No you don't!
SUSIE: [Challenging] Don't I? Why not?

DAVE: Because you are against her and it's a dangerous game!

SUSIE: I'm not against her! **[Looks anxiously at JEAN who is still apparently engrossed in her paper]** How can you say that?

DAVE: **[Pause]** …Just cut it out! …Why don't we have a game?

SUSIE: **[Confused]** What?

DAVE: **[Waves the deck of playing cards in front of her]** Cards!

DAVE takes the stool in front of the sideboard, SUSIE takes the other one. DAVE deals out cards and they start to play.

ANDY: **[To JEAN]** Anything interesting?

JEAN: Depends what you're interested in.

ANDY: Anything that catches your eye?

JEAN: "Young man, in his mid to late twenties, thrown out of a second storey window…"

ANDY: What's that?

JEAN: "…Critically ill in hospital with multiple fractures…"

ANDY: Bloody hell! Any more? Where was it? Does it say who was involved?

JEAN: "…Police say they are looking for a middle-aged woman in connection with the incident, and suspect the motive was being pissed off at not being left to read the paper in peace!"

ANDY: Oh.

DAVE: **[To SUSIE]** Well? What have you got?

SUSIE: Three jacks.

DAVE: Flush.

SUSIE: Damn!

DAVE: So, what do you know?

SUSIE: [Dealing cards for the next game] What do you mean?

DAVE: You knew more about the set-up than we did!

SUSIE: Rubbish! All I knew was what Mum told us.

DAVE: Don't come that with me!

SUSIE: It's true!

DAVE: [Leaning in close to SUSIE] I know it isn't true! And I know who you are!

SUSIE: I don't know what you're talking about!

DAVE grabs SUSIE's jumper and drags her towards him until their faces are almost touching.

DAVE: Listen to me! It would be better for you if you told me everything now! If you don't, I'll tell her [indicating JEAN with a tilt of his head] everything I suspect!

SUSIE: Look, Dad…

DAVE: Oh, forget all that crap!

SUSIE: OK, what should I call you?

DAVE: Maybe you should call me 'Sir' – until I know you better!

SUSIE: [Derisively] "Sir"? …OK! Look, I don't know what you think you know about me but, whatever it is, you're wrong. I'm in this for exactly the same reasons as the rest of you!

DAVE: [Aside] Probably true! [To SUSIE] How did you know they'd changed position?

SUSIE: I didn't know – I just guessed.

DAVE: You're a worse liar than you are a card-sharp! **[Taking a playing card out of SUSIE's sleeve]** I think you're with them! I think you've been sent here to spy on us and get word out at the first opportunity!

SUSIE: It's not true! It's not true – oh, shit! - don't tell Jean! Oh, God, please?

DAVE: It is true! What's your real name? Tell me and I'll give you a chance - hold back and I'll march you over there, right now!

SUSIE: My real name's Clare. I'm not with anyone else, I swear!

ANDY: **[To JEAN]** How long have you known Rob?

JEAN: Still asking questions? ...I've known him a damn sight longer than I've known you. ...He's done quite a few favours for me in the past. He's never the brains of the operation, but he doesn't need to be. He's the muscle I lack!

ANDY: He's a big bloke!

JEAN: You wouldn't want to get on the wrong side of him!

ANDY: I don't like getting on the wrong side of you!

JEAN: It amounts to the same thing! He's always been our best – he sorted things out for John and he stayed with me after. He's my lovely boy: ironing out the creases and breaking a few skulls...

SUSIE: **[Overhearing JEAN]** Charming!

DAVE: Shhhhh! **[Grabs SUSIE's collar and pushes her out of a door, off stage left]**

JEAN gets up from the rocking chair and sits opposite ANDY at the table

JEAN: What do you think that was about?

ANDY: Don't know, but it seemed.. ..intense!

JEAN: You're an idiot!

ANDY: Thank you!

JEAN gets up from the table and exits stage right. DAVE re-enters (stage left), and, finding JEAN has gone, sits down opposite ANDY

DAVE: Where's Jean?

ANDY: [Corrects] You mean, 'where's Mum'?

DAVE: You're an idiot!

ANDY: OK, where's Susie?

DAVE: [Corrects] Where's Clare?

ANDY: Who's Clare?

DAVE shakes his head, gets up from the table and exits stage right

ANDY: What the hell's going on? **[He wanders off in the direction of the other two]**

SUSIE re-enters (stage left), and, not seeing ANDY, sits down at the table. Making a cursory check that no-one's around, she

takes out a mobile phone and switches it on. After a few seconds it emits a loud ring in an absurd ring-tone.

SUSIE: [**Jabs at the phone**] Shhhh! Go away! Bloody messages!

SUSIE sits, listening to messages and then ends the call. ANDY enters further into the room and hovers in front of the doorway, stage right. SUSIE's mobile rings again and she rejects the call. A few seconds later, it rings a third time.

SUSIE: [**Answering the phone**] Hello? Yes. Look, I told you not to call me on this number! What's wrong? …Then why are you calling me? …That's nice. …Does anyone else there have this number? …I don't care! …That's the point – I don't want anyone finding me! …I can't tell you where I am! …I can't tell you! …OK, good! Don't call me any more! I'll be in touch with you - when I can! …And don't give anyone else this number! [**Ends the call**]

ANDY: Who was that?

SUSIE: [**Jumps and drops her phone**] Andy! Shit, you scared me! I thought it was one of the others! …It was no-one.

ANDY: Not Rob?

SUSIE: No. Why would Rob call me? He'll call Mum on the main phone. …Anyway, he won't call before five, will he?

ANDY: So, who was it? Just a friend?

SUSIE: No-one.

ANDY: Was it your boyfriend?

SUSIE: You're an idiot!

ANDY: [Sighs] So I've been told.

DAVE and JEAN re-enter through the stage right door. They brush past ANDY and sit at the table – JEAN at the head and DAVE opposite SUSIE. A long, tense silence follows

JEAN: Susie. Got anything you want to tell me?

SUSIE: Like what? What's he been telling you?

DAVE: I haven't said anything. I just mentioned you wanted a word.

SUSIE: [Aggressively] Well, I don't!

JEAN: That's no way to speak to your father!

SUSIE: Isn't it time we dropped this charade?

JEAN: No. I don't think so. I think it's a good way of doing things. Just think of this as a nice, cosy little chat with Mum and Dad.

SUSIE: Sounds ominous. Am I going to be grounded?

DAVE: That all depends on what you say. …Susie's not your real name.

SUSIE: It's not.

JEAN: I see.

SUSIE: So what? You're not using your real names!

JEAN: Let's stick with you, shall we? What is your name?

SUSIE: Clare.

DAVE: Last name?

SUSIE: I don't have to tell you that!

JEAN: Why did you lie?

SUSIE: Self-protection.

JEAN: In what way?

SUSIE: There was information about you I didn't have – I felt safer knowing you didn't know everything about me.

DAVE: Do you feel more vulnerable now that we know you're Clare?

SUSIE: Not really.

ANDY: You should!

JEAN: Shut up! ...And stop lurking in that doorway!

ANDY: What do you want me to do?

DAVE: Make yourself useful!

ANDY: Doing what?

DAVE and JEAN turn on ANDY

ANDY: OK, fine! I'll go upstairs and see if... I don't know – the toilet flushes OK. **[Turns to go out of the room, stage right. Pauses]**   Oh, you might want to listen to the messages on her mobile phone. **[Exits]**

DAVE and JEAN turn back to SUSIE

JEAN: What messages are they?

SUSIE: I don't know what he's on about. I haven't even got a mobile.

JEAN: [To DAVE] Dad!

DAVE: [Stands up, walks round the table (near the audience), to stand behind SUSIE] We can do this the easy way or the hard way...

ANDY: [From the doorway] That's such a corny line!

JEAN & DAVE:[Together] Get out!

DAVE puts his hands on the back of SUSIE's chair and puts his face down to hers. She pauses for a moment and then gets her mobile phone out and passes it to him, over her shoulder

DAVE: Thank you.

DAVE walks back to his seat, behind JEAN, giving her the mobile as he passes. JEAN turns the mobile over in her hands. She presses first one button and then another but can't switch it on

JEAN: [Passing the mobile to DAVE] You do it.

DAVE: How do you switch it on? [turning it over in his hand] It's not like the one I've got.

JEAN leans towards DAVE and they both pore over the mobile. SUSIE tries to edge her chair out, quietly, hoping to sneak off

JEAN: [Noticing SUSIE] No you don't! [She catches SUSIE's right ear and pulls her towards her by it] How does it work?

SUSIE: Ow! Mum! You're hurting!

JEAN: Good! Tell him how it works – and don't try anything or it'll hurt a lot worse!

SUSIE: OK, OK! There's a button on the top of the phone... God! This is a crazy situation! This is mad! There's nothing on there you'll want!

JEAN: I'll be the judge of that!

DAVE: It won't switch on!

SUSIE: It will! It will! You have to press the button on top and hold it in for a second or two. Let me have it – I'll show you.

JEAN: You won't! You'll tell him what to do!

DAVE: I've got it! It's lighting up. [To SUSIE] Your ear's turning red!

SUSIE looks as though she wants to reply but thinks better of it

DAVE: Alright. It's on. What do I press for messages?

JEAN: [Putting more pressure on] Well?

SUSIE: Get   into   the   menu   and   scroll   down   to "Call...something"...

DAVE: "Call something"? Technological jargon, eh? Trying to blind me with science?

SUSIE: "Call List" or "Call..." – it's the second one down after "Messages".

117

JEAN: But it's "Messages" we want! [To DAVE] She's playing us for fools!

SUSIE: I'm not! You don't want "Messages": that's just text-messages!

DAVE: "Call Register"?

ANDY re-enters and listens

SUSIE: Yes! That's it – "Call Register". What does it say when you go into that?

DAVE: [To JEAN] I can't see it properly.

SUSIE: It's OK – just go to the fourth option and press enter.

DAVE: OK. It says "ALL".

SUSIE: Press enter.

DAVE: "ALL CALL LISTS ERASED"

JEAN: What!

ANDY laughs

JEAN: What are you laughing at? [She turns towards ANDY, still gripping SUSIE's ear]

ANDY: She's got you to delete records of all the people who've called her since she got here? What else has she tricked you into? Have you even heard her messages yet?

DAVE: Do you know how to use one of these?

ANDY: Of course.

DAVE: Right, then! You come here. **[Gesturing ANDY to sit down in his place, he gets up and holds out the mobile to him]** Sit here, take this and I'll have a word with her!

ANDY walks to the table, takes the mobile and DAVE's chair. DAVE walks round the back of JEAN, taking the ear that JEAN is holding between the finger and thumb of his left hand. JEAN lets go, sits back and observes with a satisfied look

SUSIE: You wouldn't like to change ears, would you? That one's a bit sore.

DAVE lets go of SUSIE's right ear, smacks it and walks round to the chair on SUSIE's left. He pulls it out to sit almost behind her and takes her left ear with his right hand

DAVE: Only too happy to oblige. **[After a short time he laughs and lets go of her ear]**

JEAN: **[To ANDY]** Well, genius, have you worked it out?

ANDY: All you need to do is call a number and listen to the messages. I don't know how she got you to go into her call lists and erase them!

JEAN: Look, I'm getting royally pissed off with all of this! Are you going to get those messages or do I have to send for Rob? He hates being called out on a job during shop hours and he gets a bit careless when he's narked! **[to SUSIE]** Sometimes he

119

takes things too far, [to ANDY] and he doesn't always limit his attention to the intended 'interviewee'!

ANDY: I can get them! I just need the number.

JEAN: Don't you know it?

ANDY: It's not my network. [To SUSIE] What's the number?

SUSIE: You bastard!

DAVE: [Takes SUSIE's left arm, twists it behind her back and holds it there with his left hand. Then pulls her to him with his right arm across her chest] What's the number?

PAUSE. JEAN gets up from her seat, walks over to the sink unit and gets a carving knife out of the drawer. She comes back to the head of the table and stands with the knife aimed at SUSIE

SUSIE: 901! The number's 901!

ANDY: [Dials the number and hands the mobile to JEAN] You listen.

JEAN: [Putting down the knife and putting the mobile to her ear] "You have no new messages"!

ANDY: Saved messages?

JEAN: Shhh! [Listens intently]

JEAN ends the call and places the mobile in the middle of the table. PAUSE

ANDY: Well?

JEAN: No saved messages.

ANDY: She's wiped them.

JEAN: [**Heavy sarcasm**] Oh? You think?

DAVE: Shall I..?

JEAN: Just hold her there while I think what to do.

DAVE: [**To SUSIE**] Mum and Dad are very annoyed with you!

ANDY: Just leave the mobile on. Someone's bound to call her on it sooner or later.

JEAN: [**Looking at her watch**] Where's the remote?

ANDY: By your rocker.

JEAN: Get it.

ANDY returns with the remote and offers it to JEAN

JEAN: You do it.

ANDY checks through the teletext pages again

ANDY: Nothing.

SUSIE: I told you...

JEAN: [**Furiously picking up the knife and going for SUSIE**] Don't you dare! Don't you dare say another word or, so help me God, I'll...

Phone rings

ANDY: The mobile! I told you someone would call her!

SUSIE: It's not…

JEAN lunges at SUSIE with the carving knife. DAVE hauls
SUSIE back, away from the knife

JEAN: **[To ANDY but without taking her eyes of**
SUSIE, and still holding the knife towards her] You pick it up!
ANDY: **[Picking up SUSIE's mobile]** It's not her mobile.
DAVE: **[Calmly]**   Jean, it's the landline.   …Over there, on the
sideboard. …You should get it.

JEAN puts down the knife, slowly, then walks over to the
sideboard. She answers the phone. All eyes on JEAN

JEAN: Hello? …Rob? I wasn't expecting to hear from
you this soon! …Really? …That's very interesting! …We had our
suspicions. **[Looking at SUSIE]** You don't need to tell me, Rob. I
know who it is.   We'll keep her here 'til you come.   …What?
[JEAN's gaze turns from SUSIE to ANDY. DAVE and SUSIE
follow her gaze] …Thank you, Rob. I'll see you in five minutes.
…Bring your tools!

BLACKOUT

THE END

1820885

Made in the USA